Essential Histories

The Thirty Years' War
1618–1648

Essential Histories

The Thirty Years' War 1618–1648

Richard Bonney

First published in Great Britain in 2002 by Osprey Publishing,
Elms Court, Chapel Way, Botley, Oxford OX2 9LP, UK
Email: info@ospreypublishing.com

ISBN 1 84176 378 0

Editor: Sally Rawlings
Design: Ken Vail Graphic Design, Cambridge, UK
Cartography by The Map Studio
Index by Susan Williams
Picture research by Image Select International
Origination by Grasmere Digital Imaging, Leeds, UK
Printed and bound in China by L. Rex Printing Company Ltd.

02 03 04 05 06   10 9 8 7 6 5 4 3 2 1

For a complete list of titles available from Osprey Publishing
please contact:

Osprey Direct UK, PO Box 140,
Wellingborough, Northants, NN8 4ZA, UK.
Email: info@ospreydirect.co.uk

Osprey Direct USA, c/o MBI Publishing,
PO Box 1, 729 Prospect Avenue,
Osceola, WI 54020, USA.
Email: info@ospreydirectusa.com

www.ospreypublishing.com

ACKNOWLEDGEMENTS

The author generously acknowledges assistance from
the following scholars: Dr Peter Barber (British Library),
Dr David Parrott, Dr William Guthrie, Dr Geoffrey Mortimer
(who allowed consultation of his as yet unpublished Oxford
D. Phil. thesis: it is hoped that this will be published shortly) and
Daniel Stalberg.

Contents

Introduction

The Thirty Years' War began as a religious war, growing out of the struggle between German Roman Catholics and Protestants. It developed into a political contest that saw the Austrian Habsburg rulers of the Holy Roman Empire seeking to expand their control in Europe, while a number of other powers (such as Sweden) tried to limit their ambitions. France in particular (although also a Catholic power) was worried at the prospect of a Habsburg hegemony in Europe. The Papacy, Spain and most of the German princes joined the Catholic camp championed by the Austrian Habsburgs. They were opposed by the Protestant powers of Sweden and Denmark, Protestant German princes, and (after 1635) Catholic France. This line-up changed as princes changed sides. What did not change was the effect on the civilian population. Some areas of Germany were repeatedly plundered as unpaid, badly-equipped armies took what they needed from the lands they fought over. In this respect alone, the Thirty Years' War was the most devastating conflict in early modern Europe.

For there to have been a concept of a Thirty Years' War, contemporary accounts had to have been written during or after the peace negotiations which brought the conflict to an end. For example, the work entitled *A Short Chronicle of the Thirty Years German War* was published for the first time in 1648. Additionally, during earlier stages of the war, before the lapse of 30 years, contemporary writers used expressions demonstrating that they considered that the events, which began in Prague in 1618 and had continued since, constituted a single conflict, or even a single war. The diarist Jeremias Ullmann of Seifersdorf in Silesia noted at the peace in 1648 that 'the war has lasted 30 full years, carried off many hundred thousand souls, swallowed up many hundred million *florins* (*Gulden*), and produced nothing but afflicted people and desolate towns and villages.'

Though the Holy Roman Empire was subject to almost continuous warfare between 1618 and 1648, it is clear that not all of Germany was subject to warfare in the same degree; moreover, as the historian C V Wedgwood noted: 'the destructive powers of armies were infinitely less than they are now.' Though more detailed chronologies and separate phases of the war serve a purpose in facilitating understanding (see Chronology), the most important chronological division is a relatively easy one: the period of the war before 1631; and the second phase of the war, between 1631 and 1648.

Why is the year 1631 so important? First, because the Swedes led by King Gustavus Adolphus won a crushing victory at Breitenfeld in September. The effect of this victory was to open up the whole of Germany to invasion for the first time. By May of the following year, Bavaria was occupied and Gustavus' army reached Munich. This was a staggering military advance from the northern coastline of Germany, where his army had landed in July 1630. Second, in January 1631 France and Sweden signed an alliance at the Pomeranian town of Bärwalde, which linked the two countries together for 'the restitution of the suppressed Estates of the Empire'. There had been foreign intervention in the 1620s, notably from Denmark, and on a limited scale from the Dutch Republic; but from 1631 until the Peace of Westphalia in 1648 – with only a few diplomatic hiccups on the way – France and Sweden held together in a military alliance broadly in support of the Protestant powers in Germany. The Thirty

Years' War was no longer purely a German conflict but had become a European one. As such, the making of peace had, perforce, to be a European concern too, which greatly complicated and delayed the resolution of the conflict.

Hans Heberle commented in his diary on the religious aspect of the war: 'In 1619 Ferdinand II became [Holy] Roman Emperor, under whom a great persecution developed, with war, rebellion and much spilling of Christian blood …' For Heberle, without the driving ambition of the Emperor Ferdinand II (or, as historians would now contend, the advice of his Jesuit confessor Lamormaini), the continuity of the war would have been missing. Yet as Wedgwood noted: 'it was a revolt in Prague and the action of a prince on the Rhine [Frederick V of the Palatinate] which precipitated the war.'

For Wedgwood, the Thirty Years' War was a conflict with a religious core: 'after the expenditure of so much human life to so little purpose, [in 1648] men might have grasped the essential futility of putting the beliefs of the mind to the judgement of the sword. Instead, they rejected religion as an object to fight for and found others.' To contemporaries, putting the beliefs of the mind to the judgement of the sword was a relatively simple issue of defending 'truth' as it was understood by one religious confession against the 'falsehood' practised by the other. For the Scottish mercenary captain Robert Monro the war was fought 'for the promoting of Christs Gospell … for the libertie of our distressed brethren in Christ' (that is, the Protestants) and to overturn 'the yoke and tyranny of the house of Austria'. The eminent military historian Geoffrey Parker concludes: 'thanks to the paralysis of the normal political mechanisms, the personal determination or the prejudices of individuals … exerted a decisive effect on the course of the Thirty Years' War. Not all were men born to rule … Lamormaini relentlessly undermined the Habsburgs' victory [in 1629] by his insistence on the Edict of Restitution.' In the final analysis, it was a mere handful of these determined figures who 'kept the armies fighting and thus made the Thirty Years' War what it was'.

Chronology

1552	Truce of Passau. Secularisation of religious property outlawed after this date by the Peace of Augsburg
1555	Peace of Augsburg signed
1618	Defenestration of Prague: outbreak of Bohemian rebellion
1619	Elections of Frederick V as King of Bohemia and Ferdinand II as Holy Roman Emperor. Two sieges of Vienna
1620	Invasion of Bohemia and defeat of rebellion at the White Mountain. Neutrality of the German Protestant Union. Lower Palatinate invaded by Spain. Upper Austria occupied by Bavaria
1621	German Protestant Union dissolved. End of Twelve Years' Truce (Spain and the United Provinces/Dutch Republic)
1622	Spanish capture Jülich. Battles of Wimpfen and Hochst
1623	Surrender of Frankenthal. Battle of Stadtlohn
1624	Count von Mansfeld disbands army
1625	Spanish capture Breda. The Hague Alliance signed
1626	Battles of Dessau Bridge, Lutter
1627	Albrecht von gains Mecklenburg. New constitution for Bohemia
1628	Battle of Wolgast
1629	Peace of Lübeck. Edict of Restitution
1630	Invasion by Gustavus Adolphus. Dismissal of Albrecht von Waldstein
1631	Franco-Swedish and Franco-Bavarian treaties. Sack of Magdeburg. Victory of Gustavus Adolphus at Breitenfeld. Capture of Prague. Recall of Albrecht von Waldstein
1632	Battles of Rain, Alte Veste and Lützen. Death of Gustavus Adolphus
1633	Formation of the Heilbronn League. Battles of Hessisch-Oldendorf and Steinau
1634	Assassination of Albrecht von Waldstein. Defeat of Heilbronn League at Nördlingen. French alliance with the Heilbronn League. France occupies bases in Alsace
1635	Spain arrests Phillip-Christopher von Sötern, Elector of Trier. French declaration of war. Peace of Prague. Bernard of Saxe-Weimar joins French service
1636	Ferdinand II declares war on France. Army of Flanders invades France and reaches Corbie. Imperial army invades Burgundy. Battle of Wittstock
1637	Death of Ferdinand II and succession of Ferdinand III as Holy Roman Emperor. Swedish army withdraws to Torgau. Dutch recapture Breda
1638	Battle of Rheinfelden. Bernard of Saxe-Weimar captures Breisach
1639	Battle of Chemnitz. Death of Bernard of Saxe-Weimar
1640	Succession of Frederick William as Elector of Brandenburg
1641	Death of Johan Banér. Lennart Torstennson assumes command of Swedish forces in Germany. Franco-Swedish alliance for the duration of the war
1642	Second battle of Breitenfeld. Death of Cardinal de Richelieu
1643	Cardinal Mazarin becomes chief minister in France. Olivares resigns and is replaced by Don Luis de Haro as chief minister in Spain. Battles of Rocroi and Tuttlingen
1644	Battle of Freiburg. French occupy all Alsace

1645 Battles of Jankow and Allerheim.
Trauttsmannsdorf arrives as Imperial
plenipotentiary at Westphalia:
commencement of serious
peace negotiations

1646 Peace between Sweden and Saxony

1647 Franco-Bavarian Truce; later
Bavarian-Imperial alliance renewed

1648 Peace of Münster between Spain and
the Dutch Republic
Battles of Zusmarshausen and Lens.
Swedish siege of Prague.
Peace of Westphalia and end of the
Thirty Years' War (24 October).
Commencement of internal troubles
in France (the Fronde)

The making of alliances

The Peace of Augsburg signed in September 1555 affected political and religious arrangements in the Holy Roman Empire for many years and was at the heart of the issues involved in the Thirty Years' War. Hastily concluded by Ferdinand I, the brother of Charles V (who abdicated as Emperor a year later), in negotiation with the Lutheran princes led by Maurice of Saxony, this settlement was not intended as a 'peace of eternal duration' as it came to be regarded by the Lutherans. Yet, in the absence of any alternative settlement, a temporary arrangement, made provisionally in 1552 at the Truce of Passau, and confirmed at Augsburg in 1555, came to assume enormous importance for Germany. In the second half of the 16th century the Peace of Augsburg prevented an outbreak of civil war like that in France during the wars of religion. (See Essential Histories: *The French Religious Wars 1562–1598* by Robert J Knecht).

Though it guaranteed the peace at first, each side interpreted it differently, which in the long-term paralysed the German constitution. In particular, the peace guaranteed the position of Lutherans but not the Calvinists, with whom they had strained relations; Calvinists were those who followed the teachings of Jean Calvin, the French Reformer. At the time the Peace of Augsburg was drawn up, there were no Calvinist princes in the Empire. The spread of Calvinism, and the further expansion of Lutheranism after 1552 undermined the basis of the peace, for the Catholic princes were determined to oppose such gains. The Protestants demanded confirmation of the terms of the Peace of Augsburg at the Imperial Diet (the meeting of the German Princes) held at Regensburg in 1608. When the Catholics offered confirmation of the Peace, subject to a return of all ecclesiastical property 'secularised' (that is, with Lutheran or Calvinist administrators) since 1552, the elector of the Rhine Palatinate and other hard-line Calvinist princes withdrew from the Diet. There was a second Protestant walkout at the next Diet held in 1613. The Imperial constitution was deadlocked and the prospects for a peaceful resolution to the political and religious disputes were gravely diminished. The Imperial Diet was not summoned again until 1640.

Frederick V (1596–1632), elector of the Rhine Palatinate (1610–23) and king of Bohemia (1619–20) after Van Dyck. (Ann Ronan Picture Library)

Royal Palace at Hradcany, where the Defenestration of Prague took place on 23 May 1618. (AKG, Berlin)

Though an outbreak of war had seemed very likely in 1609–10 over the future of the Cleves–Jülich succession, in the end, it was events in Bohemia in 1618, not those in Cleves–Jülich in 1609, which proved to be the stimulus for the outbreak of a sustained German war. Encouraged by the leadership of the Protestant Union, the Calvinists in Bohemia were pressing for a comprehensive interpretation of the concessions granted to Protestants at a time of political weakness by Emperor Rudolf II in the Letter of Majesty in 1609. Ferdinand of Styria, the future Emperor Ferdinand II, elected king of Bohemia in July 1617, was in no mood to grant these privileges; educated by Jesuits, he had vowed to eliminate heresy in his patrimonial lands. Though he at first confirmed the Letter of Majesty, Ferdinand had no intention of acknowledging Protestant equality in Bohemia. Protestant churches were destroyed at Braunau

(Broumov) and Klostergrab (Hroby). The 30 official guardians of Protestant rights, the 'defensors', led by Count Matthias Thurn, threw two representatives of Ferdinand out of a 70-foot-high window of the Royal Palace at Hradcany, Prague: this act, known to history as the Defenestration of Prague (23 May 1618) launched the Thirty Years' War. Subsequently, the Bohemian estates deposed Ferdinand as their king by a majority decision (19 August 1619) and elected in his place Frederick V of the Palatinate (26 August).

However, Ferdinand held other titles in addition to Bohemian and the Austrian lands. He was elected king of Hungary in 1618 and ruler of Germany (Holy Roman Emperor) on 28 August 1619. Once Emperor, Ferdinand II could outlaw his enemies for treason or breach of the peace of the empire and offer the lands and titles which were forfeited to reward his allies. The Bohemian rebels contended that they had seized the crown not from an emperor but from an Austrian archduke. This was technically correct, since Ferdinand II had

ABOVE Philip III, king of Spain (1578–1621, king from 1598). [Velázquez, 1599–1660] (AKG, Berlin)

RIGHT Maximilian, Duke and from 1623 elector of Bavaria (1573–1651; duke from 1597). Leader of the Catholic League. (AKG, Berlin)

not been elected emperor at the time of his deposition in Bohemia. However, he had dominated the Imperial government since July 1618, so there could be no doubt against whom the revolt had been directed.

At a subsequent meeting of the Imperial electors held in March 1620, Bohemia was declared an integral part of the empire. The logic of this decision was that the Bohemian rebellion might become part of a greater struggle within the empire and, if defeated, Frederick V might be driven out of Bohemia and also be deprived of his lands and titles in Germany. The future of the Counter-Reformation in Germany and the autocratic ambitions of the emperor were interdependent. The fear in the Thirty Years' War was that Ferdinand II's notorious vow to eliminate heresy in his patrimonial lands might be applied to the empire as a whole.

However, the military events of 1618 and 1619 demonstrated that Ferdinand II was not strong enough to crush the Bohemian rebellion without assistance. In August 1618, the rebels had received support in the form of a mercenary army (recruited by the Duke of Savoy) under the conduct of Count Ernst von Mansfeld, an experienced commander and illegitimate son of a governor-general of the Spanish Netherlands. The city of Pilsen in eastern Bohemia had remained loyal to the emperor. In the autumn of 1618, von Mansfeld's forces moved against it, and on 21 November 1618, after several weeks of siege, the town fell: this was the first major military event of the war and the images of the siege were duly reported.

Apart from the Papacy, which could be counted on to back the Catholic dynasty, Ferdinand II had three main potential allies: Spain, Bavaria and Saxony. Of these allies, Spain was crucial because in 1618 Philip III of Spain (1598–1621) was the only ally with both military and financial resources at his disposition. The Duke of Lerma, who served as chief minister for most of Philip III's reign, sought to keep the peace;

but his influence was on the wane. Oñate, the Spanish ambassador at Vienna, and Zúñiga (Lerma's rival for power as chief minister) were in the ascendary and wanted to make a decisive stand for Bohemia. As a result of their influence, Philip III pronounced that 'Germany cannot possibly be abandoned.' A massive recoinage of the Castilian currency had been ordered in 1617 and loan contracts (*asientos*) to the record value of 8.6 million *ducats* were signed in 1619. The resources for a major campaign in northern Europe and financial support for Ferdinand II was secured.

The forging of an alliance with Maximilian of Bavaria (1597–1651) was a second course of action open to Ferdinand II, although it was not bought cheaply. Maximilian understood that Ferdinand's resources had been gravely weakened by the rebellion: he therefore insisted that he should be compensated for the costs of military intervention by military occupation of the Archduchy of Austria, or parts of it, until he was reimbursed. The formal agreement between the emperor, Spain and Bavaria was sealed in the treaty of Munich of 8 October 1619. However, in a secret condition, Maximilian also demanded substantial parts of the Palatinate and that the electoral title should be transferred to his branch of the Wittelsbach dynasty. The second demand was formally conceded in February 1623 (for the lifetime of Maximilian only), but in the event, because of the size of the debt (some 16–18 million *florins*) Bavarian troops remained in occupation of Upper Austria until 1628.

The third ally involved against the Bohemian rebellion was Saxony. John George of Saxony had rejected an offer to be elected king of Bohemia; but he was unlikely to allow his Protestant rival – a Calvinist – to gain Bohemia in his place. Commencing a trend that would continue up to the 1640s of Lutherans refusing to co-operate with Calvinists in the general Protestant cause, John George accepted a guarantee from the emperor which appeared to safeguard secularised church lands in the Upper and Lower Saxon circles ('circles' or *Kreise* were defined areas in Germany for the purposes of military recruitment). He also received the Margravate of Lusatia and Silesia in pledge for the repayment of his costs in joining the war effort on the side of the Habsburgs. It was, in one sense, an 'unholy' alliance combining Catholic and Lutheran forces; but few would have been ignorant of the fact that in 1546–47 it was precisely with such an alliance of Catholics and Lutherans that Charles V had defeated the Lutheran rebellion of the Schmalkaldic League. In October 1620, John George captured Bautzen, the capital of Lusatia, after only minimal resistance. The pincer movement had been launched, and the Bohemian rebellion was isolated and trapped by the diplomatic alignment of 1619–20.

Protestant divisions and unifying issues in the Catholic alliance

At the battle of Nordlingen in 1634, the rallying cry of the joint Spanish and Austrian Habsburg forces was *Viva la casa de Austria!* The German war was not solely a war of religion, since politics, dynastic and state interests were inseparable aspects of it. The religious bond alone could not hold armies together but it could provide important additional cement. The Catholic League army under Bavarian command was not quite a Bavarian territorial army. Traditionalist Bavarian Catholics rallied behind the army of the Catholic League, marching under standards with images of Mary and Jesus, and increasingly in the Wittelsbach colours of blue and white. Hostility to Protestantism – especially Calvinism – was a unifying factor in the uneasy coalition against the foreign policy of Frederick V of the Palatinate. There was, moreover, undoubtedly a religious aspect to the armies' favourable treatment of towns. When Straubingen was taken by Bavarian forces in 1634, 'the Duke of Bavaria pillaged not the towne, for that the Burgers were all Papists, who by flinging of letters over the wal[l]s, had both discovered the weakness of the garrison to the besiegers, and invited them after three repulses received, to fall on againe.'

Yet military exigency counted more than religious loyalty in the attitude of commanders towards the occupied population. The Swedish commander Karl Gustav Wrangel instructed the town commandants of Triebsees, Demmin, Loitz, and Anklam to allow the victims of plundering to recover their goods and property, permitting them to enter the camp in order to identify their horses, cattle, and possessions. All exports of cattle and horses from the region were temporarily halted to ensure compliance with his orders. In contrast, Johan Banér argued that if the 'contributions' had been paid promptly the soldiery would

not have committed abuses: 'I do not believe that the Imperialist troops, when they occupied this land a number of years ago, behaved much better,' he commented, 'or that the land was better protected then than now … God forbid that they should once again rule the land in this way.'

The Imperialist and Catholic cause in the Thirty Years' War had a number of significant advantages over the Protestant alliances. The first was that of legitimacy. Emperor Ferdinand II may not have possessed a significant army of his own at his accession in 1619, but he was able to use the legal instruments at his disposal to outlaw the rebellion of Frederick V, and to dispose of his territories and even electoral title. The legality of some of his measures was certainly contested, especially the implementation of the edict of restitution in 1629. Yet there were strong German national sentiments, which tended to rally around the emperor in time of crisis. As the French plenipotentiaries at Westphalia reminded Cardinal Mazarin, Chief Minister of Louis XIV, in 1645 the Germans were 'touched … by the love of their country and cannot accept that foreigners dismember the empire'.

Until 1648, under the laws of the empire, negotiations with foreign powers and the right of war and peace rested with the emperor. Ferdinand II was thus able to exploit such sentiments to rally to his side Lutheran princes such as John George of Saxony in 1620 and again in 1635. The princes were not sovereign powers and thus, according to the laws of the empire, had no right of contracting alliances with foreign powers. The alliance of Maximilian of Bavaria with France in May 1631, for example, was technically illegal – as well as of little immediate help against the Swedish onslaught. However, there was nothing to stop the emperor contracting such treaties with foreign powers: here the family alliance between the Austrian and Spanish Habsburgs was to prove vital in 1620 and again in 1634. If the alliance proved of less help to Ferdinand III than it had to his father, it was because the French diverted most of their resources to the Franco-Spanish conflict in the Low Countries which kept the Spaniards fully occupied in the late 1630s and 1640s. Nevertheless, for the first half of the German war, it seemed likely that the emperor would win, and Maximilian of Bavaria, for one, was convinced that co-operation with the emperor was the best way to achieve his goals. However, it is important to draw the correct inference from this tripartite alliance, which formed the cornerstone of the early Catholic victories in the Thirty Years' War. French strategy under

Mazarin believed that if Bavaria insisted on peace, the emperor would have to follow, and that Spain would follow the emperor because it would not wish to fight on alone. This linkage was incorrect: in 1647 the emperor was prepared to fight on without Bavaria, which eventually rallied once more to Ferdinand III's cause, while in 1648 nothing would induce Spain to make peace with France. In the end even the informal Habsburg family alliance could be broken if the strategic interests of Spain and the Austrian lands diverged.

Emperor Ferdinand III (1608–57; emperor from 1637). Engraving in 1649 depicting him (erroneously) as victor in the war and peace-giver to Germany. (University of Leicester)

Advantages of the Catholic alliance system

Apart from the political and constitutional advantages for the Catholic cause of the tripartite alliance of the Holy Roman empire, Spain and Bavaria, there were two other distinct gains from this continuity in policy. The first was what seemed an inexhaustible supply of Spanish funds and troops to underwrite the Austrian Habsburg cause at critical moments, such as in 1620. The second advantage was an equally critical supply of experienced field commanders. The multinational and polyglot Spanish Habsburg armies provided the training ground for commanders in the Thirty Years' War, and what Spain did not provide Bavaria was able to supplement. With the exception of Albrecht von Waldstein (1583–1634), genuinely 'Imperial' commanders – commanders who had risen through the ranks and were battle-hardened in earlier conflicts – were few and far between. Waldstein was first and foremost a logistical genius, the greatest of the breed of entrepreneurial mercenary captains, rather than a proven commander at the highest level. He had relatively little battlefield experience, despite his title of generalissimo. Spínola, Count Tilly, Pappenheim, Waldstein, von Mercy, and von Werth were all competent, or even outstanding, commanders on the Habsburg/Catholic League side. Of Count Tilly (1559–1632), Guthrie comments: 'it was Tilly's bad luck to face Gustavus Adolphus at his military peak at a time when he himself was past his prime.' Pappenheim (1594–1632) was considered the best cavalry commander in Germany. As long as the outcome of battles tended to depend on the quality and number of veteran troops in service, the Bavarian and Imperial armies tended to perform well in the Thirty Years' War.

The rapid, if temporary, collapse of the Catholic predominance in Germany after the battle of Breitenfeld is difficult to explain. The deaths of Tilly and Pappenheim in 1632 and the disfavour and subsequent murder of Waldstein in 1634 consolidated this collapse, but they did not precipitate it. Guthrie attributes the chief explanation to a 'massive loss of confidence' on the part of the Imperial and League forces, a panic spreading from the lowest trooper right up to Elector Maximilian and the emperor. 'The long run of victories from White Mountain to Magdeburg had conferred upon Tilly and his army an aura of invincibility. The total, irretrievable destruction of this reputation was a greater blow than any merely military reversal.'

The weakness of the Catholic position became more evident in the later stages of the war, when Spain was preoccupied with the French offensive in the Low Countries and the Swedish began a sustained campaign to strike a blow at the resource base of both the Austrian Habsburgs and Bavaria. In 1641, Emperor Ferdinand III stated that the war from 1618 to 1640 had already cost his hereditary lands, the *Erbländer* –that is, Bohemia, Moravia, Silesia, Upper and Lower Austria– more than 71.4 million *florins*, which represented more than a century's worth of pre-war revenue and still did not account for the full cost of the war. Maximilian of Bavaria expended some 12 to 14 million *florins* in supporting the emperor in the campaigns of 1619–22. The total expenditure of Bavaria and the Catholic League between 1620 and 1652 amounted to more than 58.8 million *florins*. Of this total, the army costs amounted to 43.2 million, with another six million for provisions and 1.3 million for Bavarian militia and garrison costs. How much income was raised remains a matter of conjecture but, for the years 1619–48, one estimate is 38.5 million.

Albrecht von Waldstein (Albert of Wallenstein), Duke of Friedland (1583–1634), Imperial Generalissimo. (AKG, Berlin)

Ambrosio Spínola, Marqués de Los Balbases (1569–1630),
Spanish commander in the army of the Netherlands and
commander in Germany. (Ann Ronan Picture Library)

Johannes Tserklaes, Count of Tilly (1559–1632), experienced and successful commander of the Catholic League army. (Ann Ronan Picture Library)

The Protestant alliance system

The Protestant cause had none of the advantages of legitimacy, powerful foreign support or significant financial assistance that nurtured the Catholic party before 1631. It was fatally divided between Lutherans and Calvinists; the latter being, on the whole, considerably more aggressive in their political standpoint than Lutherans, such as John George of Saxony, who were naturally inclined to seek an accommodation with the emperor. The earlier commanders in the 1620s – Ernst von Mansfeld, Christian of Brunswick (1599–1626) and George of Baden-Durlach (1573–1630) – lacked strategic and organisational competence and the Protestant armies:

organised on [the principle] of small units, complex deployments and prescriptive drill suffered a virtually uninterrupted series of defeats stretching from the White Mountain to Wolgast, leading to the consequent annihilation of Protestant military power in Germany by the later 1620s.

Denmark under Christian IV lacked sufficient resources, financial and military, to sustain its intervention. England in the 1620s, as later on in the German war, proved a broken reed and was effectively neutral, despite the wishes of Parliament and James I's family relationship with the Elector Palatine, he was father-in-law to Frederick V.

The significance of the Swedish intervention in Germany

The fluctuations in Swedish military fortunes in Germany after 1630 account, in large measure, for the changing military balance between the Catholic and Protestant sides. Gustavus Adolphus had landed at Peenemünde in June 1630 with just 14,000 troops, far short of the 46,000 men he intended, but by September the army was strengthened to around 26,000. From then on, there was a continuing Swedish military

presence in Germany until after the end of the war. At the beginning of 1632, the Swedish forces in Germany consisted of 83,000 men, a force that in February to March 1632 had risen

further to 108,000 men. Of these troops, 13,000 were Swedish and Finnish, the rest were mercenaries. The Swedish and Finnish proportion is reduced further if we take into

Christian IV, king of Denmark (1577–1648; king from 1588). His military intervention in Germany suffered a drastic setback in his first campaining year, 1626. [Karl von Monder, 1640]. (AKG, Berlin)

account Sweden's allies from Mecklenburg, Bremen, Saxony and Brandenburg, which increased the total forces under Gustavus Adolphus' command to 140,000 men.

What made the Swedish military intervention in Germany unique was the military genius of Gustavus Adolphus. In Monro's opinion he was 'both head and heart of the kingdom' ... 'the Master of Military discipline, being risen from a prentise, to the great professor of Arts, in this eminent and high calling of a souldier'. Military specialists contest Monro's verdict in detail; for Guthrie, Gustavus was 'not a systematic siege engineer; his methods relied heavily on aggressiveness, assaults, bluff, good luck and dazzling displays of artillery expertise'. Yet Guthrie concedes that he was:

the pivotal figure of the Thirty Years' War, the leading military innovator of his time, a brilliant tactician with considerable operational ability. As a strategist, however, he was no better than average, and his grasp of logistics was frankly poor. The king was seen by Protestants as a saviour, and his amazing personal charisma won admirers everywhere.

In terms of both his strategic vision and the political possibilities of bringing about a settlement favourable to the Protestants, Gustavus Adolphus was irreplaceable. For all his political skill, Axel Oxenstierna – the chancellor of Sweden after 1612 and director of the Swedish war effort in Germany after Lützen in 1632 – could not provide the military co-ordination or aggression of the late king. Without the continued Swedish commitment after the defeat at Nordlingen, the Protestant cause would have been decisively overthrown and the Peace of Prague of 1635 might have become a permanent settlement. At times it seemed that the Swedish position in Germany was on the verge of collapse, only for a spectacular recovery to be achieved.

Part of the weakness of the Swedish position was financial. There was never any prospect of central revenues from Sweden

Gustavus Adolphus, king of Sweden (1594–1632; king from 1611). The 'Lion of the North' and Protestant champion. (AKG, Berlin)

underwriting the war effort in Germany: Swedish revenues were insufficient for this to be possible. On the contrary, the war effort was supposed to pay for itself: as Gustavus Adolphus put it, war must 'sustain war' by military success: once an army had devastated the land it had occupied, it must move on to new territory where it could repeat the process. Fluctuations in the size of the mercenary force undoubtedly account for part of the recurrent difficulties of the Swedish army in Germany. When numbers fell to 10,000 men or so, it could no longer seize territory and supply itself; to gain quarters an army of 25,000 men was much more useful. As the Vicomte de Turenne

Axel Oxenstierna, Chancellor of Sweden (1583–1654; chancellor from 1612). Gustavus' faithful collaborator and custodian of his legacy. (AKG, Berlin)

the later 1640s because of its political importance: the Austrian homelands. If the emperor suffered the occupation of his own territories, then conceivably he would be forced to make peace. This explains the Saxon occupation of Prague in 1631 after the battle of Breitenfeld and the Swedish attacks on Prague in 1639 and 1648 and, above all, the general search for winter quarters in Bohemia.

Protestant commanders

Gustavus Adolphus left behind a cohort of remarkable captains. Bernard of Saxe-Weimar saved the day at Lützen in 1632, but later transferred to French service. In Guthrie's verdict he 'was an able, aggressive officer, an above average strategist and operationally good, but he lacked judgement. Determination won him more battles than he lost.' Gustavus Horn, Marshal of Sweden (1592–1657) was steadier and less remarkable but was captured at Nordlingen and not released until 1642. Gustavus Adolphus had also trained the great offensive generals in the period of adversity and later resurgence: Johan Banér (1596–1641), Lennart Torstennson (1603–51) and Karl Gustav Wrangel (1603–76), the first two being among the handful of men whom the late king had trusted.

expressed it: 'nothing provides quarters in Germany except an army as strong as that of the enemy.' The more land that could be seized as quarters for the Swedish army, the less land was available to the Imperial army. If the Swedish army was forced back to its bastion of Mecklenburg and Pomerania, it faced starvation. Movement was what was needed. The advantage of Franco-Swedish military collaboration was that it increased the total army size to 25,000 men or more and allowed for a war of mobility, the consolidation of territorial gains and the search for winter quarters in Germany. One area was singled out for particular attack in

Torstennson was the greatest Swedish artillery specialist. It was crucial to the outcome of the Thirty Years' War that though the Swedish army suffered some reverses in the 1640s no important defeat was inflicted; instead, defeats were all on the side of the Imperial–Bavarian alliance. Two decisive factors throughout the war were Swedish morale and the superiority of its cavalry formation: on several occasions, these turned the tide of battle in their and their allies' favour. In the later stages of the war, the decisive advantage in size and skill of the Swedish artillery force – which was apparent at Wittstock (1636), Breitenfeld (1642) and Jankow (1645) – helped carry the day. In this respect Jankow, with a Swedish superiority of 34 cannon, is the classic example.

Swedish artillery innovations

Sweden had a well-established armaments industry. Its portable cannon were used to good effect at various stages of the war and to crushing effect at the first battle of Breitenfeld in 1631, where the Swedes had a 51:27 superiority in standard cannon; in addition they had the advantage of four mobile batteries attached to each regiment, raising the total to 75:26, though the large guns were stationary for most of the battle. Turner commented that 'the Swedish Trains of Artillery since their first footing in Germany have had the reputation to be the most exactly composed, and conducted by the most experimented Artists of any in Christendom.'

By the time of the battle of Jankow in 1645, the Imperialists blamed their defeat on the almost total Swedish 60:28 artillery superiority, assisted by the fact that the Imperial army lost half its artillery and most of its ammunition early on in the battle. Daniel Staberg comments that the Swedish artillery was 'probably the best in Europe in 1645, highly trained and experienced with excellent equipment and munitions'. As commander of Gustavus Adolphus' artillery, Torstennson had played a large part in the late king's reforms of the artillery, reforms that he continued in the decade 1635–45. He redesigned the 12-pounder and its carriage in order to improve mobility as well as finishing the development of the 'regimental gun'. Torstennson raised an artillery regiment of two companies that was transported to Germany in 1635. This regiment had eight 24-pounders; 14 12-pounders; and 49 three-pound regimental guns. The larger part of this force joined the main army, and the number of guns (71) is very close to the number (70) given for the second battle of Breitenfeld in 1642.

At Jankow the Swedish artillery was able to keep up with the army's movement as a result of the frozen ground and extra team-horses. Even the heavy 24-pounders were brought into action despite the gun barrels being transported separately from their carriages. A battery of guns was moved through forest and deployed at the forest edge in order to fire into the flank of the Imperial army. The regimental guns were generally deployed in support of the infantry brigades but they were also able to form independent batteries as required during the battle. One important factor was that the regimental artillery fired 'cartridged' ammunition, that is, the cannonball was wired to the charge, which increased the rate of fire to four or six shots a minute. This important innovation seems subsequently to have been forgotten at the end of the war and had to be 'rediscovered' by the Swedish artillery commander Cronstedt in 1710.

The French military effort

As a result of its superior population and fiscal resources France was in a unique position to alter the balance of power in the German war by permanently tipping the scales against the emperor. Yet without doubt, after an initially strong strategic position was gained in Lorraine and Alsace between 1632 and 1634, the French army consistently underperformed in Germany. There were two main reasons for this. The first was that the north (Spanish Netherlands) and north-eastern (Lorraine) frontiers of France consistently absorbed the largest proportion of the French manpower and resources after 1635. There were occasional victories in the Spanish Netherlands, such as at Rocroi in 1643 and Lens during 1648. These were less important in terms of the damage they inflicted on Spain than any defeat, followed by Spanish invasion, would have been to France during a royal minority, such as after 1643. The northern front was, in David Parrott's view, a 'clumsy, uneconomic and ill-conceived way of trying to force the Habsburgs to terms, and one which drained away the possibility of achieving more decisive results in other campaign theatres'. Mazarin, Chief Minister of the young Louis XIV, was of the opinion that, by obtaining winter quarters in the empire, the French army would free up money for use on the northern front against Spain.

Unlike the Swedes, it was unrealistic for the French to seek winter quarters in the Austrian Habsburg lands, such as Bohemia. French quarters were taken instead in Franche-Comté until the declaration of its neutrality in 1644, or in Swabia. As a result of the French priority of confronting the Spanish in the Low Countries, their armies in Germany were relatively small, with inferior cavalry components to the 'normal' ratio of 40 cavalry to 60 infantry, and they were starved of artillery. With such limited resources at their disposition, it is striking that de Guébriant, Louis de Bourbon, prince of Condé and Turenne managed to secure the relative successes in Germany that they did.

French regiments were smaller than the 'norm' in Germany: 1,200 men rather than the more usually cited figure of 2,000 men. For a few weeks in the crisis year

of 1636, Parrott estimates that the government 'may have been maintaining 70,000–80,000 infantry and 10,000–15,000 cavalry' but this was 'probably the highest real total achieved during either the ministries of Richelieu or Mazarin,' that is, an absolute maximum of 95,000 men. For the rest of the time, French 'troops on campaign numbered no more than 70,000–80,000 in total' while there is no evidence of any significant reserve of garrison troops in France itself.

Infantry forces in the Thirty Years' War

Pikemen, considered the elite of the infantry, were the essential component of any 17th-century army, since the bayonet had not been developed to protect musketeers from cavalry charges. Alongside the heavy cavalry (cuirassiers equipped with horse trappings, wheel-lock pistols and a broadsword), lighter units developed, whose members wore a half cuirass, and carried a wheel-lock carbine as well as a cavalry sword and wheel-lock pistol. These troops were initially referred to as 'arquebusiers', and after the introduction of the carbine as

Estimates of comparative force size in the later battles of the Thirty Years' War				
Battle	**Army**	**Infantry**	**Cavalry**	**Cannon**
Wittstock 1636	Imperialist	8,500	10,122	30
	Swedish	7,730	10,250	60
Second Breitenfeld 1642	Imperialist	10,000	16,000	46
	Swedish	10,000	10,000	70
Rocroi 1643	Spanish	18,000	5,050	18
	French	14,400	6,400	12
Freiburg 1644	Bavarian	8,300	8,200	20
	French	11,000	9,000	37
Jankow 1645	Imperialist	5,000	11,000	26
	Swedish*	6,135	8,530	60
Second Nördlingen 1645	Bavarian	8,800	7,200	28
	French	7,800	9,200	27
* Plus 452 gunners and 900 officers = 16,017 total.				

Source: W. P. Guthrie, *Battles of the Later Thirty Years' War* (forthcoming at Greenwood).
The author is indebted to Dr Guthrie for his helpful comments and assistance and for providing this table, which he regards as 'best estimates'.

'carabineers'. Under the celebrated Spanish *tercio* formation, the pikemen could be variously arranged. In the classic formation of 3,000 men, 1,500 pikemen were placed at the centre in a formation of 56 lines, each of 22 pikemen with two surrounding cover parties each of 125 arquebusiers. The rest of the arquebusiers were deployed in four units *(mangas)* of 240 men. Two groups, each of 90 musketeers, were deployed at the front on either side of the arquebusiers. Another formation was called 'the wide extension' (*El prolongado de gran frente*), while a simpler formation was nicknamed 'the gentleman' (*El gente*), respectively for *tercios* of 1,450 men, 650 pikemen and 800 musketeers and 1,740 men, 800 pikemen and 960 musketeers. The effectiveness of the Spanish *tercio* resulted from the

co-ordination of different weapons, but above all from the maintenance of strict discipline, effective training and the capacity of the commander to form mobile combat groups from the *mangas*. Variants of the *tercio* formation used in Germany (called *Gevierthaufen*) included the Imperial *tercio* of 1,024 men, 512 each of pikemen and musketeers and the League *tercio*, favoured by Tilly of 2,028 men, 968 pikemen and 1,068 musketeers. The latter ensured crushing superiority in the early battles of the Thirty Years' War before Breitenfeld, from the White Mountain in 1618 down to Wimpfen, Hochst, Stadtlohn and Lutter. It was impervious to attack and shatter thinner formations. Each *tercio* essentially moved and fought on its own: mutual support of the units was difficult, if not impossible, to co-ordinate.

In campaigning terms, the crushing Swedish victory at Breitenfeld in 1631 was, in Guthrie's phrase, 'a historical watershed'.

Surrender of Breda to Spínola, 2 June 1625. [Velázquez] The Spanish title of the painting is *Las Lanzas.* (Ann Ronan Picture Library)

After Sweden's entry into the war the less deeply echeloned 'Swedish order of battle' gained importance. This was experimental, with a difference between theory and practice and evolved from Breitenfeld and Lützen. One scheme had 96 officers and 504 troops, divided between 216 pikemen and 192 musketeers, with a force of 96 musketeers kept back as a reserve to lend assistance when necessary. However, its success depended heavily on the discipline and inner unity of the troops: unlike the Danish army, the Swedish army under Gustavus Adolphus was already battle- hardened through its campaigns in Polish Prussia.

Sir James Turner, an English commentator, thought that the Swedish success spelt out the death of the pike in battle. After Gustavus entered Germany, 'Pikemen were still accounted the Body of the Infantry', yet after his victory at Breitenfeld 'the Pikemans' defensive Arms were cast away, and after them the Pike itself, insomuch that all who hereafter were levied and enrolled, called for Muskets.' Turner's view was doubtless exaggerated. But he also pointed to the multiple lines of musketeers, as many as six, in the Swedish army who could 'fire all at once by kneeling, stooping and standing', and thus acting almost as a battering ram. The Swedish army employed more musketeers than pikemen, in approximately a 2:1 ratio. The reasons for the preference of musketeers to pikemen were fairly straightforward: it was much less expensive to equip a troop of musketeers compared to a troop of pikemen and the weapon was less heavy on a forced march.

The German war cost Sweden some 50,000 mortalities. All able-bodied men between the age of 15 and 60 were conscripted almost every year for military service. Swedish nationals were the most trustworthy part of the 'Royal Army' in the Baltic coast garrisons, where they secured the lines of both supplies and retreat, and they fulfilled vital functions in battle. A further socio-political consequence of the crown's

policy of donations to reward its military and civilian personnel during Sweden's war of expansion was the shrinking supply of crown property, tended by free farmers. This process progressed at an accelerated rate under Queen Christina and was only partially reversed in the form of 'reductions' starting in 1650.

The 'Swedish' army at Jankow in 1645 was almost completely made up of German units commanded by German and Swedish officers. The only 'national' Swedish troops were 500 Swedish and Finnish infantry and the majority of the artillerymen. There is no evidence about the ratio of pike to shot, but the number of pikemen was probably low, with many companies and regiments being completely armed with muskets. The few remaining pikemen were without armour, since the Swedish government stopped issuing armour in 1635–36. By 1645 the infantry tactics introduced by Gustavus Adolphus were no longer in use, the 'Swedish brigade', and salvo fire combined with charges were all a thing of the past. Instead the troops had adopted the less complicated

Christina, Queen of Sweden (1626–89; r. 1632–54). (AKG, Berlin)

'German system' and had lost much of their former aggression. Infantry combat tended to be dominated by long and indecisive fire fights, while the outcome of battles was decided by the cavalry battle on the flanks. At Jankow the morale of the infantry was high and most of the soldiers and officers were veterans, their quality and training being shown by their ability to deploy and redeploy in the face of the enemy and to enter a battle after a march, regroup and fight a new battle during the same day.

Gustavus Adolphus' attempt to provide uniforms for the soldiers was abandoned with the possible exception of national Swedish regiments. The infantry are often depicted in ragged clothing of mixed colours in contemporary art. The infantry of the various armies normally wore wide trousers and a jacket-like jerkin with wide sleeves. Coats were largely unknown, possession of footwear was often the exception. As Bernhard Kroener observes: 'the general diversity of appearance made additional distinctive features necessary, in order to distinguish friend from foe during battle. Allied troops tried to make themselves recognisable by quickly breaking off green twigs and attaching them to their clothing. During battle, as the mass streamed to and fro in chaos and gunsmoke and dust greatly reduced vision, these signs were not particularly effective. In such situations flags, standards, and battle cries were most likely to give the soldiers a degree of orientation.'

The relatively high personnel losses, whether due to the direct effects of war or, to a much greater extent, through hunger and epidemics brought in its wake, resulted in a rapid decrease in the size of regiments, making the merging of units unavoidable. A soldier did not automatically change company, for in many respects it was a substitute for home life. Regiments reflected the structures of local loyalties of the recruiting area in which they were raised. Among the troops raised on the territory of the empire only a relatively small percentage (10–20 per cent) of the soldiers were from non-German-speaking areas.

Cavalry, dragoons and the food supply

Swedish forces

At the victory at Nordlingen in 1634, the joint Habsburg forces outnumbered the Protestants both in absolute numbers and in numbers of cavalry. The Swedes had a total of 25,700 men, of whom only 9,700 were cavalry, and in addition, there were, 1,000 dragoons. The Habsburg forces in contrast, had 33,000 men, of whom 13,000 were cavalry. At Jankow in 1645 the Swedish cavalry had increased in number, totalling 8,530 men compared with 6,135 infantry; but it should be noted that, though the Imperial cavalry was more numerous at 11,000 men, their side still lost the battle. While overall numbers had increased, the Swedish regiments and squadrons had become weaker in strength.

Stalberg notes that armour had been abandoned to a varying degree with the best-equipped units retaining only back- and breast-plate and an iron skull cap underneath the hat. Helmets and heavier armour are no longer seen in depictions of common troopers, though the documentation is scarce since units were no longer equipped by the Swedish state. Buffcoats were popular but expensive items and their use was limited among the common troopers.

The cavalry retained the tactics of Gustavus Adolphus' reign, and generally charged at the trot, firing their pistols just before or in the actual mêlée. The Swedish cavalry did not charge at the gallop until the 1670s, when some officers introduced the French *charge en sauvage*. Poorly-equipped units may have charged with sword alone and at a higher speed but the evidence for this is limited. As with the infantry, the Swedish cavalry at Jankow was a well-tested and highly experienced force since cavalry suffered less from attrition than infantry in the later stages of the war. The best regiments were probably the Livonians and Courlanders who had begun their service as cuirassiers in the army of Gustavus Adolphus in the late 1620s. The Courlanders were commanded by Karl Gustaf, later Charles X, the second of the great Swedish 'Warrior kings'.

Kroener notes that 'as extremely mobile mounted infantry, the dragoons attained special importance during the war. They made it possible to carry out surprise attacks, and their supply profited from their greater radius of movement.'

Other troops

Mounted arquebusiers existed in the French army in the form of regiments of carabins, sometimes referred to as *fusiliers à cheval*. Although these are sometimes viewed as early dragoons, they are perhaps better regarded as more of a cross between Imperial-style arquebusiers and mounted infantry, and they were able to perform their duties on horseback as well as dismounted. Unlike the Swedish and Imperial dragoons, they were not dressed as infantry; instead they wore the standard cavalry buffcoat and helmet (sometimes with back- and breast-plates as well) and were armed with a pair of pistols in addition to their sword and flintlock carbine.

Armies were encumbered by their baggage train and as food became scarcer the longer the war went on, the deployment of smaller mobile military units gained greater importance alongside the regular large-scale battles. The last years of the war were characterised by the capture of fixed points, to guard road routes and river crossings and also as centres from which the surrounding area could be foraged for supplies. Raiding parties deployed for this purpose were mobile mounted units. Initially they contributed to reconnaissance of the enemy's strength and position, later also establishing and securing march routes and quarters with favourable supply situations.

As the main task of these light troops became tracking down food supplies, seizing enemy convoys and taking magazines, their discipline slackened. They were deployed far ahead of the army or on its flanks. The prospect of looting without punishment

led not only to scattered troops, but also convicted soldiers and armed desperadoes to make war on their own account as 'freebooters' (*Freireuter*). Contemporaries often associated these feared and dreaded soldiers with the Croat regiments which served the emperor: these *Crabaten* were blamed for many of the atrocities of the war. There were similar prejudices against soldiers from other regions of Europe.

Food rations

Soldiers were entitled to a daily ration of 730 grams of bread, two-thirds of wheat and one-third of rye flour; two days' rations were supposed to be baked in one loaf and distributed. But the men rarely received the amount or quality promised and regional differences in weights and measures often provided a cover for the fraudulent reduction in the weight of the ration. If this failed to raise the supplier's profit margin, bread was made with inferior grain like barley, vetch was added or bran was mixed with water. Officers sometimes took bribes directly from the suppliers, while others presented provisions lists which included as recipients those who had deserted, been captured by the enemy, or were dead. It was always the soldiers who suffered. Gnawing hunger, which the soldiers often tried to deaden with alcohol, was commonplace. Poor nutrition and sanitation in the camps repeatedly caused many serious cases of dysentry in the armies of the Thirty Years' War.

While the bread rations were supposed to be delivered directly to the soldiers, meat, beer, wine and cider had to be purchased at the camp market. Butchers and cooks were accused of increasing their profit margins by using poor-quality or maggot-contaminated meat and mouldy pulses, and by adulterating beer and wine. If the soldiers were paid late – more the rule than the exception – or the army's luck ran out, cooks and army suppliers (sutlers) disappeared overnight because there was no longer any prospect of gaining a profit. The wise commander knew how to turn an occasional issue of pay to his advantage, making it seem more a reward than an entitlement, 'knowing well how hungry men could be contented with little, in time of neede', as Monro said of Gustavus Adolphus. Those who had joined up expecting to get regular pay were doomed to disappointment. Turner sardonically commented that the soldiers were called mercenaries, 'but if you will consider how their wages are paid, I suppose, you will rather think them Voluntaries, at least very generous, for doing the greatest part of their service for nothing'.

The Bohemian rebellion, 1618–1620

The Defenestration of Prague launched the Bohemian rebellion, but it was the acceptance by the elector Palatine, Frederick V, of the throne on 26 August 1619 and his subsequent coronation in November of that year that transformed a conflict into a war. The native Palatine advisers had concluded that 'acceptance [of the Bohemian crown] would bring a general religious war', but had been overruled by the advice of Christian of Anhalt and Ludwig Camerarius, who urged acceptance.

The rebellion was hopelessly divided along religious, political and social lines. Lutherans refused to co-operate with Calvinists, nobles with townsmen and Frederick V soon found that his actions rapidly eroded the early support he had enjoyed. Maurice, Count of Nassau, stadholder in Holland and captain-general of the United Provinces, was willing to provide 50,000 *guilders* (25,000 *thalers*) per month subsidy to his nephew Frederick, with the aim not just to protect Protestantism in Bohemia but also to divert the attention of the Habsburgs to Central Europe. It is thought that this subsidy and a number of Dutch regiments provided about an eighth of Frederick V's troops in Bohemia. But otherwise the rebels were short of funds. When Moravia joined the rebellion in June 1619, its erstwhile infantry commander, Albrecht von Waldstein, the future Imperial generalissimo, fled to Vienna with the receipts of the Moravian treasury. The help came at a vital moment, because the rebel forces under Count Matthias Thurn marched through Lower Austria and began a desultory siege of Vienna, which was abandoned a few days later on 14 June. The rebels lacked sufficient artillery to sustain the siege and their lines of communication were disastrously overextended.

Though most of his Austrian lands joined the rebellion (the exceptions were Styria, Carniola and the Tyrol), Ferdinand II had at his disposal greater resources in money and troops. In May 1619, a force of 7,000 veterans from the Spanish Army of Flanders moved across the empire to Vienna to assist him. By July, he had received 3.4 million thalers in financial assistance from Spain. With the aid of these subsidies, the Imperial army numbered some 30,000 men. On 10 June, Count Bucquoy, Ferdinand II's experienced general from the Low Countries wars, commanded a victorious force which crushed von Mansfeld's troops at Záblatí in southern Bohemia: some remnants of his cavalry escaped, but the infantry force was totally wiped out. It was an inauspicious background to the offer of the crown to Frederick V.

Help came to the Bohemian rebellion from an unexpected quarter: Transylvania. After 1613, Transylvanian policy under its ruling prince (*voivode*) Bethlen Gábor was to establish a Protestant alternative for Hungary by military force and alliances with foreign powers, including the Ottoman Turks. Ferdinand II was deposed as king of Hungary and Bethlen Gábor was elected king by the Diet in the summer of 1620 in the presence of an Ottoman delegation; Sultan Osman II authorised the Diet to elect a king 'well disposed' towards him. 'Calvino-Turkism' in Hungary inevitably meant a policy directed against Habsburg, and Catholic interests. The surprising feature of Bethlen Gábor's programme, however, was his willingness to extend his sphere of influence abroad.

After defeating the last Habsburg army in Hungary on 13 October 1619, and before consolidating his political position there, Bethlen Gábor and his Transylvanian forces moved up the Danube and joined forces with

Thurn's army in November to besiege Vienna a second time. But on 27 November, Bethlen Gábor received news of an invasion of Upper Hungary by Poland and was forced to withdraw from the siege. Subsequently, on 20 January 1620, he accepted an Imperial offer of a nine- month truce, which left him in temporary possession of his Hungarian conquests. In spite of two later appearances, this set the pattern for Bethlen Gábor's interventions in the Thirty Years' War: a series of treaties – Nickolsburg (1621), Vienna (1624) and Pozsony (1626) – extricated him from the German war while preserving the Hungarian status quo in constitutional and religious terms.

Transfer of the conflict to Germany

On the eve of Ferdinand II's crushing victory of the Bohemian rebellion and the transfer of the conflict to German soil, the main European powers, with the exception of Spain were unprepared for the conflict. In the later stages of the rebellion neither of the Baltic participants – Denmark and Sweden – were overly concerned with developments in far away Bohemia. Sweden was about to begin an era of expansion with Gustavus Adolphus' offensive against Poland in 1621; Denmark would seek to exploit any weakness of its Baltic rival. The Dutch were preoccupied with overcoming their internal political dissensions and with preparations for meeting the challenge presented by the expiry of the Twelve Years' Truce with Spain in 1621, which was certain to lead to renewed fighting. The subsidy to the Bohemian rebels was only continued in the face of severe opposition from the inland provinces in the Dutch Republic. James I of England had no intention of supporting his son-in-law's cause by armed intervention and sought to establish his own credentials as a mediator between the opposing sides.

At this time there was no European power to act as a check on Spanish policy in 1620. It

Emperor Ferdinand II, (1580–1637); emperor from 1619. (Roger-Viollet)

is true that Zúñiga, Philip III's chief minister, was gloomy both about the prospects of renewed war with the Dutch, but as Ronald Asch comments:

In many ways the Elector Palatine had chosen the worst possible moment for a confrontation with Ferdinand. On the one hand Spain had already decided to give her interests in central Europe a higher priority than in the preceding years and to prepare for a renewal of the war in the Netherlands, but on the other hand the war had not yet started again, so that the Spanish monarchy still had enough resources available to support Ferdinand in Bohemia and in Germany.

Philip III's council became convinced that the most effective way to assist Vienna was to mount a diversionary attack on the Lower or Rhine Palatinate. This would free up Bavaria to intervene in Bohemia, without any fear of attack from the rear. For Philip III, it would carry an additional possible benefit, in that under a treaty signed with Ferdinand II in March 1617 financial and military support from Spain was conditional on the cession of Alsace. The prospect of such a transfer would be heightened by direct Spanish intervention.

The critical event which precipitated war in Germany was the Treaty of Ulm (3 July 1620), paradoxically, the very settlement by which French mediators sought to prevent a German conflict. The renewal of civil war in France in 1620 and 1621–22, and the unresolved nature of the conflict between the crown and the Huguenots, precluded an active French foreign policy before 1624, and even then French ambitions were directed towards Italy rather than Germany. Despite tacit support for Ferdinand II's position, the Treaty of Ulm was supposed to be followed up by French mediation in the conflict between the emperor and the Bohemian rebels. However, the French negotiator, the duc d'Angoulême, was told that, in the emperor's view, there was 'nothing more to be gained from treaties'; he was 'resolved to secure complete obedience from his subjects, and this could only be assured by the sword'.

The folly of the French position in allowing Ferdinand II this initial advantage was fully revealed. The forces of the Catholic League were free to assist the emperor in Bohemia, while those of the Protestant Union were left in Germany to offer such resistance as they could to the Spanish invasion of the Rhine Palatinate. Within a fortnight of the Treaty of Ulm, a Catholic League army of 30,000 men under Johannes Tserklaes, Count Tilly, marched into Upper Austria, which had sided with the Bohemian rebellion. The army of John George of Saxony marched into Lusatia and Silesia. With the exception of Bautzen, the capital of Lusatia, which was taken in September after a short siege, the rest of the campaign was relatively bloodless. The conditions of the

Saxon occupation were less harsh than those suffered by Bohemia, and the Silesian Estates managed to obtain guarantees for the survival of Protestantism. To the west, Philip III did not wait for the defeat of the Bohemian rebellion. Spínola's invasion and occupation of the Lower or Rhine Palatinate began in September, a full four months before the Imperial sentence (or 'ban') was pronounced against Frederick V in January 1621. Most of the Spanish advance was secured by capitulations; only Frankenthal, Mannheim and Heidelberg, whose defence was bolstered by the presence of English volunteers, held out against Spínola.

Collapse of the Bohemian rebellion

As for Bohemia itself, the definitive battle occurred at the White Mountain about five miles west of Prague, on 7 November 1620. The numbers were evenly matched, 24,800 men, comprising 18,800 infantry and 6,000 cavalry on the Catholic side as against 23,000 men, comprising 11,600 infantry and 11,400 cavalry on the Protestant side, but the Catholics had superior organisation and a much higher proportion of veteran troops. Christian of Anhalt had superior numbers of cavalry, but they were essentially light cavalry, 'more suited to raiding than battle' in Guthrie's judgement. The joint Imperial–Bavarian army under Counts Bucquoy and Tilly routed the rebels in a two-hour engagement. Some 4,000 men were killed on the Protestant side, as against Catholic losses of 800; 100 standards and all the 10 field guns of the Protestants were captured. The Bohemian rebels had been crushed. It remained for the linked rebellion in Germany to meet a similar fate.

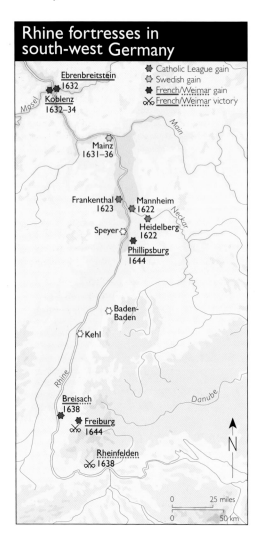

Rhine fortresses in south-west Germany

♣ Catholic League gain
♧ Swedish gain
♣ French/Weimar gain
✄ French/Weimar victory

Ebrenbreitstein 1632
Koblenz 1632–34
Mosel
Main
Mainz 1631–36
Frankenthal 1623
Mannheim 1622
Speyer
Heidelberg 1622
Neckar
Phillipsburg 1644
Baden-Baden
Kehl
Rhine
Breisach 1638
Freiburg 1644
Danube
Rheinfelden 1638
N
0   25 miles
0   50 km

War in Germany, 1621–1648

The war for the Palatinate

In the Palatinate phase of the Thirty Years' War, between 1621 and 1624, the supporters of Frederick V tried to regain the lands that he had lost so ignominiously in the early stages of the war. They were not assisted by the dispersion of the German Protestant Unión on 14 May 1621; under the terms of the Mainz Accord of 1 April it had agreed that its army would be disbanded if Spínola guaranteed its right as a neutral in the conflict. On 25 October 1621, von Mansfeld's troops arrived to relieve Frankenthal from the besieging Spanish. Von Mansfeld spent the winter of 1621–22 ravaging Imperial territory after Tilly's forces occupied the Lower Palatinate. In the meantime, George of Baden-Durlach raised an army of 11,000 men in his territories, while Christian of Brunswick raised a further army of 10,000 men in Lower Saxony.

The death of Philip III in March 1621 and the succession of his son Philip IV failed to alter the determination of Spain: it was, if anything, increased by the formidable energy of Gaspar de Guzmán – Count-Duke of Olivares, and Zúñiga's nephew – Chief Minister until January 1643. He was determined to prevent any loss of authority which might result from a slackening in Spanish Habsburg military commitments in Europe and subscribed to a 17th–century version of the 'domino theory': 'after Germany would fall Italy,' he pronounced, 'and after Italy, Flanders, then the Indies, Naples and Sicily.' The logic of the policy was one of total commitment, the gradual move from a series of small wars to a general European war.

In February 1622, Spínola forced the surrender of the Dutch garrison of Jülich. On 6 May, George of Baden-Durlach was defeated

Gaspar de Guzmán, Count-Duke of Olivares (1587–1645) Chief Minister of Philip IV (1622–43). [Velázquez] (AKG, Berlin)

at Wimpfen by the joint armies of Spain and the Catholic League (under Tilly) while trying to cross the River Neckar. Tilly's victory was the result of a daring strategy and superior numbers; he had 13,000 infantry and 5,000 cavalry against 9,400 infantry and 3,300 cavalry in Baden-Durlach's army, enjoying a 3:2 advantage. Some 2,000 Protestants were killed and 1,100 captured after the battle but, though two-thirds of Baden's army escaped, it was badly demoralised and no more than 3,000 men rejoined von Mansfeld's army. Furthermore, Christian of Brunswick was intercepted and defeated at Höchst, on 20 June, by the Spanish and Catholic League armies, while trying to cross the river Main in order to join von Mansfeld on the southern bank of the river. On this occasion, the Catholic armies totalled about 22,000 infantry and 12,000 cavalry, but no more than 18,000 and 10,000 respectively were actually engaged in the battle; Christian of Brunswick had 13,000 infantry and 8,300 cavalry and suffered heavy losses, with the remaining troops declared a rabble by von Mansfeld.

On 19 September, Tilly accepted the surrender of Heidelberg after an 11-week siege. The capitulation of Mannheim followed on 2 November, while in March 1623 Frankenthal surrendered to the control of Archduchess Isabella of the Spanish Netherlands. The victory of Tilly and the Catholic League over the forces of Christian of Brunswick at Stadtlohn on 6 August 1623 has been called the 'most decisive' of all the Catholic victories to date in the Thirty Years' War. Tilly's army was both more numerous than that of Brunswick and also of superior quality. Eleven of Brunswick's 20 regiments were newly formed, while even the veteran units were heavily diluted with raw recruits. Guthrie calls Stadtlohn 'Tilly's most complete victory'. The losses on the Protestant side were crushing: 6,000 or 7,000 of Brunswick's men were killed, 4,000 were captured and the rest scattered; yet the total Catholic losses, killed and wounded, came to less than 1,000 men.

By August 1623, Frederick V had lost everything. He had been deposed as elector by the emperor on 23 February. Two days later, Ferdinand II ceded the vacant electoral title to Maximilian of Bavaria for his lifetime. In July 1624, the validity of this transfer was recognised even by the Lutheran John George of Saxony. Tilly's army was left as the master of north-west Germany, except for east Friesland, which was occupied by the Dutch, while in January 1624 even the inveterate campaigner von Mansfeld disbanded his army. There was no fighting in Germany in 1624, demonstrating that the Thirty Years' War was not quite a continuous conflict, at least in terms of the fighting. The Protestant cause seemed doomed to failure, while in the later Westphalian peace negotiations Catholics were reasonably content to accept the year 1624 as the starting point for determining the religious status quo in Germany.

The Danish intervention

This was the inauspicious background to the period of Danish intervention in the years 1625–29. At Lüneburg in May 1625, the Diet (*Kreistag*) of the Lower Saxon circle elected Christian IV of Denmark director (*Kreisoberst*) of the circle, he was a member of the 'circle', or military defence area, because of the lands he held in Germany, chiefly Holstein. A later meeting of the Diet at Brunswick resolved on war, but there was a fatal delay: it was not until 9 December that The Hague Alliance was formed, comprising England, the Dutch and Denmark. Under the terms of this treaty, Christian IV was required to maintain an army of 30,000 infantry and 8,000 cavalry in the field, while the English undertook to pay a subsidy of 300,000 *florins* per month, and the Dutch 50,000 *florins*. While the Protestant alliance proved slow to establish itself, the Imperial and Catholic League forces were given time to respond to the challenge. On 15 July, on the orders of Maximilian of Bavaria and with the consent of the emperor, Tilly crossed the river Weser and entered the Lower Saxon circle. In September, Waldstein moved his army of 20,000 from northern Bohemia and marched west to Germany. This army took its winter quarters in the rich Protestant bishoprics of Halberstadt and Magdeburg.

It was not until the spring of 1626 that the campaigning came to a head. On 25 April Waldstein relieved the siege of a fortified position held by his lieutenant, Aldringen, and routed von Mansfeld's besieging troops at Dessau Bridge on the river Elbe. 'The efficient use of superior numbers to eliminate a weaker opponent was to become something of a Waldstein speciality,' writes Guthrie. Von Mansfeld had less than 7,000 men against an Imperialist army of at least double the size. Having lost nearly half his forces due to Waldstein

Peter Ernest II, Count von Mansfeld, Protestant mercenary captain (c1580–1626). Engraving after a portrait by van Dyck. (University of Leicester)

capturing 3,000 men, mostly infantry, von Mansfeld and the remnant of his army took up quarters in Brandenburg. He moved on into Silesia with reinforcements in June; in October, a truce was reached between Waldstein and von Mansfeld, but this did not help the Protestant commander's position. During the following campaigning season, in May 1627, having occupied the line of the Elbe, Waldstein rapidly cleansed Upper Silesia of the remnants of von Mansfeld's armies.

On the western front, Tilly captured Göttingen on 5 August 1626 and on the 27th confronted the forces of Christian IV at Lutter-am-Bamberg. Christian IV's army was outnumbered by Tilly's forces, which had been reinforced by some of Waldstein's soldiers seconded to his service, and the Danes were heavily defeated. Losses were far greater on the Protestant side: 3-4,000 troops were killed, some 2,500 captured and 2,100 deserted – mostly joining Tilly's army. Tilly reported 200 League troops dead, 300 seriously wounded and 200 Imperialist troops lost. Lutter-am-Bamberg 'was probably

Tilly's greatest victory', comments Guthrie, while Christian IV's 'prestige had suffered an irreparable blow, and the German princes were eager to make what terms they could'. The following May, having completed his operations on the eastern front, Waldstein turned westward to join up with Tilly's forces and occupied the Mecklenburg duchies. On 14 September 1627, Danish Holstein was invaded and the last Danish field army was annihilated at Grossenbrode.

On 14 December, Christian IV was forced to withdraw to the Baltic islands. The title of 'Admiral of the Baltic Sea' was conferred on Waldstein by the emperor in January 1628; on 11 March, he also received the duchies of Mecklenburg with the key ports of Wismar and Rostock. It remained only for Waldstein to flush out support for Christian IV and the Protestant cause from the islands off the north German coast in the following campaigning season. Yet this proved a much more difficult enterprise than expected. The proposed 'Imperial Armada' was a plan rather than a reality. On 4 February, Waldstein dispatched von Arnim to garrison Stralsund in Pomerania. The Stralsunders

The recruitment of children (Anwerbung von Kindern), by Christian Richter; 1642. (Staatliche Grsphische Sammlung Meiserstabe 10, München)

sought the protection of Gustavus Adolphus in a 30-year alliance signed on 23 June. The siege of Stralsund began on 13 May, and on 6 July Waldstein arrived to conduct the siege in person. Remarkably, given their tradition of rivalry, Sweden and Denmark co-operated to ensure its defence. On 24 July, Waldstein was forced to lift the siege of Stralsund. This gave Sweden its first foothold on the German mainland.

Waldstein's bloodied nose at Stralsund was of no assistance to Christian IV's cause. On 2 September, Waldstein crushed the Danish forces at Wolgast (*Wolgastum*), forcing Christian IV to take refuge by ship and withdraw to Denmark. The outcome was disastrous for the Danish attempt to become a significant power in north Germany. It was a foregone conclusion that Christian IV would be obliged to withdraw from the war, although the Peace of Lübeck was delayed until 7 July 1629.

The war might have ended there, with a modicum of statesmanship on the part of Ferdinand II, had he disbanded his army and been satisfied with the gains made for Catholicism in Germany as a result of the rout of the Protestant Union, the Palatinate and its foreign protectors. That the war did not end there was the result of the disastrous decision taken in March 1629 by the emperor, under the influence of his Jesuit confessor, Lamormaini, to promulgate the Edict of Restitution.

The Edict of Restitution and Swedish intervention

The edict represented the Catholic view that the secularisation of church lands after 1552 was illegal and that only those Protestants adhering to the Confession of Augsburg of 1530 (that is, Lutherans) were included in the provisions of the Peace of Augsburg of 1555. The upshot was that Calvinism was proscribed as a religion in the empire and five bishoprics and about 30 free cities were reallocated between the Habsburg and Wittelsbach dynasties. Even Catholic electors expressed

doubts about the legality of the edict, though not the policy it enshrined. At their electoral meeting at Regensburg in August 1630, they forced the dismissal of Waldstein as Imperial generalissimo, refused to elect Ferdinand II's son as king of the Romans (apparently questioning the Habsburg automatic right of succession to the Imperial title) and, most significantly, reduced the size of the Imperial army (from 150,000 men on paper to 39,000 men; the League army was also reduced to 20,000 men), altering both its command structure and method of finance. Count Tilly was appointed commander of both the Imperial and Catholic League armies, but was required to keep the two military command structures distinct and separate.

The electoral reaction to the threat of Imperial autocracy was understandable; but the timing was particularly unfortunate for the Catholic cause. Shortly before the electors' decision to force the dismissal of Waldstein, the empire found itself in a new war: the war of Swedish intervention, which lasted from 1630 to 1635. Throughout the 1620s, Gustavus Adolphus had been embroiled in an expansionist war in Poland; this came to a temporary end in 1629, and enabled him to turn his attention elsewhere with the assistance of a war subsidy conceded by Poland.

What did Gustavus Adolphus hope to achieve by intervening in Germany? Axel Oxenstierna, Chancellor of Sweden during the reigns of Gustavus Adolphus and Christina, recalled after the king's death that he had aimed at first only 'to ensure the safety of his kingdom and the Baltic, and to liberate the oppressed lands' in Germany. Yet Oxenstierna also affirmed that 'it was no part of his original intention to press on as far as he did.' The ultimate success of the Swedish invasion took everyone, including it seems the king, by surprise. The Swedish invasion began on 6 July 1630, when Gustavus Adolphus and his army arrived at Peenemünde on the island of Usedom. On 10 July, Stettin, capital of Pomerania, was occupied by the Swedish army. In January 1631, Gustavus Adolphus occupied most of Mecklenburg. The process of slow but steady Swedish gains was jolted by a

Gustavus Adolphus, king of Sweden, killed at Lützen on 16 November 1632. *The Swedish Intelligencer*, a contemporary newsletter, reported his dying words: 'I am the King of Sweden, who doe seale the Religion and Libertie of the Germane Nation with my blood.' (Roger-Viollet)

in what constituted the single worst atrocity of the war and certainly the event that was most widely recorded. Practically the whole city was destroyed by fire and 24,000 men, women and children are said to have died. The city had been the sole ally-in-arms of Gustavus Adolphus since 1 August 1630, when it had sought to break free from the re- Catholicisation programme following the Edict of Restitution.

Revenge for those who suffered at Magdeburg was a factor in the escalation of atrocities during the war. On 6 August 1631, Tilly attempted to follow up his pyrrhic victory by attempting to storm Gustavus Adolphus' fortified camp at Werben, but he was repulsed. Gustavus had long realized that the security of Sweden demanded a firm alliance with Pomerania, Brandenburg and preferably Saxony. John George of Saxony was formerly the ally of the Emperor and was always likely to be a reluctant and inconstant ally of Gustavus. However, the mere indication that John George was adopting a neutral, 'third force', position and seeking a compromise peace (which might be seen as an anti-Catholic and anti-Imperial policy) was sufficient to goad Tilly into a pre-emptive invasion of Saxony. As Guthrie comments,

setback on 20 May 1631, when the army of the Catholic League, under Tilly and Pappenheim, captured and sacked Magdeburg,

Siege of Magdeburg, 20 May 1631. (AKG, Berlin)

'Tilly was not alone in considering John George a fool, but he erred in equating this with weakness. The elector did not back down at this show of force, in fact he went into open rebellion.' On 11 September, Saxony formally joined the Swedish–Brandenburg alliance, a week after the invasion began. Three days later, Tilly's army stormed the fortress of Pleissenburg (which guarded Leipzig) and entered the city the following day.

First battle of Breitenfeld

On 17 September 1631, Gustavus Adolphus won a crushing victory at Breitenfeld, just north of Leipzig, 'the first major Protestant victory in the field since the war began' (See map on p.46). This was the largest set-piece battle of the war, with 40,000 to 42,000 troops on the side of Sweden and Saxony (there were some 14,842 infantry and 8,064 cavalry in the Swedish army, though perhaps 75 per cent were Germans or Scots mercenaries; and some 13,000 infantry and 5,225 cavalry in the Saxon army) and 31,000 men under Tilly (21,400 infantry and 10,000 cavalry). Indeed, the battle was unique in its scale until the 1660s. Tilly lost over a third, but probably less than the frequently- cited figure of two-thirds, of his army through death in battle, injury, capture or desertion. The Swedes captured 19 cavalry standards and 80 infantry colours, far more than their meagre haul at Lützen the following year. How had this spectacular Swedish success been achieved?

There were clearly short-term as well as more structural, longer-term reasons for the Swedish victory that followed five hours of desperate fighting. The three armies – Imperial-Catholic League, opposing Swedish and Saxon– had all placed their infantry in the centre and flanked it with cavalry at the wings. Unlike the other two, however, the Swedes were drawn up in a novel formation of two distinct lines with a substantial reserve of cavalry and infantry behind them plus a reserve of cavalry behind the second line. In the centre were four infantry brigades, each with six regimental cannons. At the front

PRÆLII.

INTER

SÉRENISS: SUECOR:
REGEM ET SAXONIÆ
ELECTOREM NEC NON
CATHOLICÆ LIGÆ GENE
RALEM COM: A TILI VII.
SEPTÉMBER ANNI MDCXXXI

PROPE LIPSIAM COMMISSI,

of the entire force, in the centre, 12 heavy cannon were drawn up in one large battery. The cavalry was divided with 4,100 horse on the right wing, and 2,300 on the left. The right wing had 1,200 musketeers, the left 800. Spaces between the infantry brigades

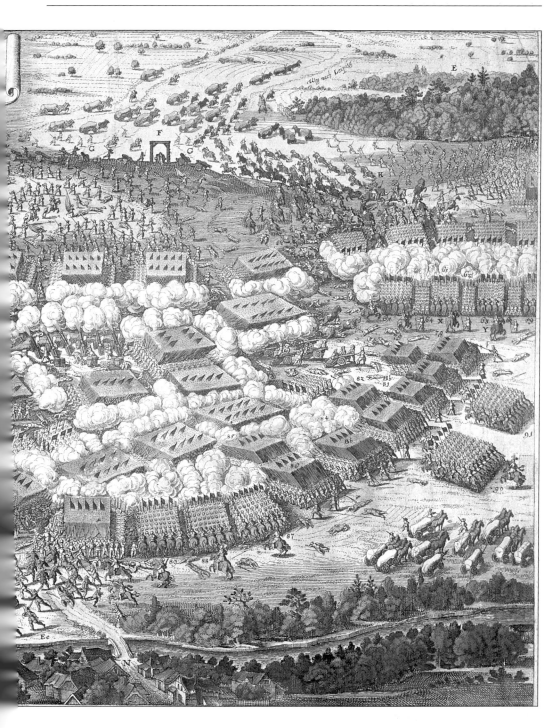

First Battle of Breitenfeld by Matthäus Merian. (AKG, Berlin)

were allowed so that squadrons of reserve cavalry could pass through, with three squadrons of cavalry as the reserve on the right. In contrast, the Saxon battalions were formed of 1,000 men drawn from regiments of variable size, and there was only one line and apparently no reserve. Opposing these armies, Tilly placed most of his cavalry on the wings, although some cavalry was placed to the rear

The first battle of Breitenfeld, 17 September 1631

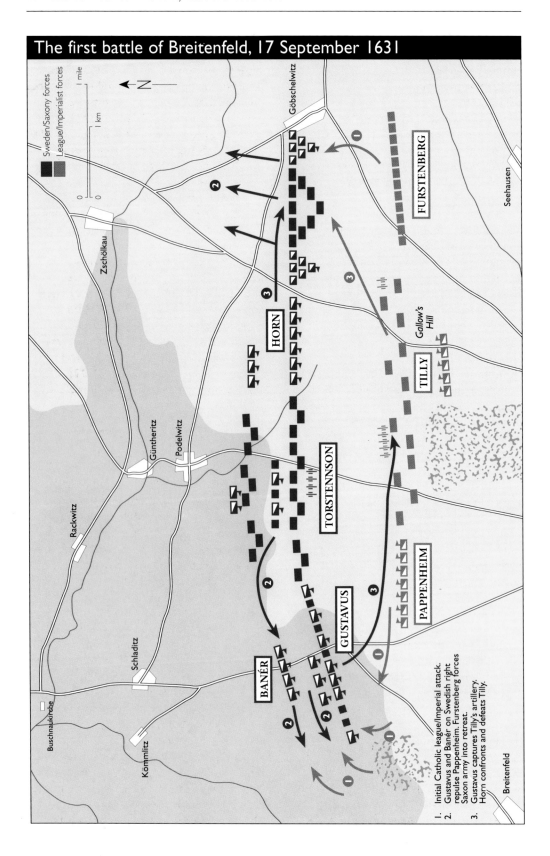

Sweden/Saxony forces
League/Imperialist forces

1 mile

1 km

←N—

Göbschelwitz

FURSTENBERG

Seehausen

Zschölkau

HORN

Gallow's Hill

TILLY

Güntheritz

Podelwitz

Rackwitz

TORSTENNSON

PAPPENHEIM

Schladitz

BANÉR

GUSTAVUS

Buschaukirche

Kömmlitz

Breitenfeld

1. Initial Catholic league/Imperial attack.
2. Gustavus and Banér on Swedish right
    repulse Pappenheim. Furstenberg forces
    Saxon army into retreat.
3. Gustavus captures Tilly's artillery.
    Horn confronts and defeats Tilly.

of the centre. The cannon was concentrated in the middle, where there were also four groups of three *tercios* each with a spare *tercio* on each flank. Each *tercio* comprised 1,500 men, probably 50 at the front and 30 deep.

Tilly attacked first, with an advance of *tercios* against the Swedish–Saxon line. His aim was to crush the opposing army between two flanking movements, as he had done at Wimpfen in 1622. Pappenheim, commanding the cavalry on the Imperial left, sought to turn the Swedish right; but he found Gustavus Adolphus, who could be reinforced as required from the reserves, trying to outflank him. The combination of musketeers, cavalry and regiment cannons presented Pappenheim with insuperable problems and high losses. Tilly's veteran infantry force of 21,000 men or so, however, made slow but definitive progress against the Saxon forces and in the end routed them. Once the Saxons had fled, Tilly turned on Gustavus Horn's small Swedish force of some 4,000 men: if the Swedish left front had collapsed, the risk was that the whole of the Swedish army would have been encompassed in the disaster. It did not. Horn was successful in reinforcing his forces, and led an early assault on the oncoming threat. Timing was of the essence: Tilly's *tercios* had not yet had the opportunity to regroup after routing the Saxons and in turn began to retreat. Meanwhile, after driving Pappenheim's forces from the field, Gustavus Adolphus was able to wheel inwards and capture Tilly's central artillery position. The Swedes used these guns on the retreating Catholic League *tercios*. The remarkable fact about this victory was that it had been achieved by under half of the Swedish army. The central infantry units had taken little part in the action, apart from holding firm and linking the two wings.

Modern commentators stress that the Imperial disaster at Breitenfeld was largely a consequence of Tilly's overconfidence in the superiority of his troops: he placed his entire army in a single line, enabling him to concentrate a formidable shock against the Swedish-Saxon army. This proved sufficient almost to gain victory by defeating the demoralised and inexperienced Saxon forces.

Gustavus Adolphus' experiences in Poland had led him to join three or four squadrons together to form a brigade, which had greater cohesion and striking power, unlike the smaller units used by the German Protestants, which had been defeated in all the contests down to 1631. In the end, it was the elite military spirit of the Swedish brigades that won Breitenfeld for Gustavus. The Saxons buckled under the pressure, the Swedes did not.

David Parrott has commented that Breitenfeld was precipitated 'because of the need to expand the contribution-base of his own army and to deny Tilly the opportunity of using Saxony for the same purpose'. He considers that the aftermath of the battle was 'a clear instance of the influence of logistics upon strategy'. More recently, William Guthrie has agreed that logistics were a constraint on Gustavus' and Tilly's actions, but argues that they were 'not the driving force. Secure occupation of fortified bases and relative numbers were far more important.'

Campaigning between Breitenfeld and Lützen

After Breitenfeld, Gustavus and the main Swedish army pushed westward through Franconia, Thuringia and down the valleys of the Main and Rhine. In November he besieged Frankfurt-am-Main and by December his troops entered the Lower Palatinate, crossing the Rhine on the 17th, 'an unprecedent feat', in Guthrie's estimation, 'winning the admiration of all Europe'. He took up winter quarters in the electorate of Mainz, building a vast military camp, called Gustavusburg, as the base for his conquering army. This strategy of Gustavus Adolphus provoked acute difficulties with France. By the terms of the treaty of Bärwalde (23 January 1631), France had undertaken to provide 400,000 *thalers* per annum for five years to subsidise Sweden's war for German liberties and the freedom of Baltic trade. Yet France remained committed to the creation of a Catholic, anti-Habsburg bloc in south Germany, one indication of which was the signature of the treaty of Fontainebleau between France and Bavaria (8 May 1631). The Swedish king's decision to seek winter quarters in the electorate of Mainz prejudiced the more general objectives of French policy towards Germany.

Worse was to come in the campaigning season of 1632, for Gustavus began operations with the siege of Donauwörth in Bavaria (16 March). On 15 April, near the city of Rain, his army crossed the river Lech in the face of heavy fire from Tilly's army; the redoubtable Tilly was mortally wounded by cannon fire in this engagement. On 17 May, Gustavus' army captured Munich, the Bavarian capital, after Elector Maximilian I had fled to Salzburg and Habsburg protection. Swedish military power was at its apogee at this moment: the king had marched his army to the south-west and then the south-east of the empire, about as far from the original landing point on the Baltic coast as it was possible to conceive. For a time in 1632, Gustavus may have had as many as 140,000 men under arms in his armies and garrisons in Germany, a wholly exceptional circumstance for Sweden, and one which was never repeated.

Yet at the very moment of its greatest triumph, the seeds for the dissolution of Swedish power had already been sown. The emperor had recalled Waldstein at the end of 1631 with the task of recruiting a new army and on 13 April 1632 he was reappointed as generalissimo. By mid-May, Waldstein had recaptured Prague and by the end of the month, the Saxon army was driven from Bohemia. On 9 June Gustavus reached Nuremberg, giving orders for new fortifications to be constructed outside the city in the form of a continuous line of earthworks and redoubts; by mid-July, Waldstein's army had begun the siege, intending to starve out the Swedish resistance. During the following two months, the supply potential of the region was exhausted. The construction of the Swedish fortified camp proved a grave error, since Waldstein was able to cut their supply lines; the error was compounded by the arrival of a relieving army. Parrott comments, 'the destruction of half of the Swedish army before Nuremberg owed little to the specific failure to capture Waldstein's positions, far more to the confinement of 45,000 troops' in too restricted an area.

On 31 August the Swedish army tried to break out of the trap by attempting to seize the Alte Veste, an old fortification on a hill just outside Waldstein's lines, but it failed to do so despite repeated assaults. Epidemics began to take hold in the overcrowded Swedish encampment. Thereafter, Waldstein sought to disperse his army rather than suffer its dissolution through his own growing supply difficulties. He captured Leipzig on 1 November, informing Pappenheim that 'if the elector [of Saxony] is lost, the king [of Sweden] must be lost too'. He considered Gustavus' army 'totally ruined' by the experience at Nuremberg. Then, bizarrely, on 14 November he concluded that the campaigning season was over and began to disband his forces.

Battle of Lützen

This accounts for the fact that the momentous battle of Lützen, which was fought all day long on 16 November 1632, took place between armies of comparable size, about 18,000 men each. The Swedish force of 18,996 men comprised 12,786 infantry and 6,210 cavalry with 60 cannon; the Imperial force initially totalled 16,770 men, comprising 9,870 infantry and 6,900 cavalry with 38 cannon, but it was later reinforced by Pappenheim's cavalry force of 2,300: there was thus a small but distinct Imperial advantage in cavalry. The tactical problem for Gustavus was to dislodge Waldstein from the defensive position he had chosen, and to do so quickly before Pappenheim's relieving force could arrive. If the enemy's left flank could be turned, then Waldstein's line of retreat to Leipzig and Bohemia would be severed. Therefore the right wing of the

Swedish army had to be reinforced with the elite troops, with the king in command. It seems that Waldstein had expected the king to attack the strongest rather than the weakest point of the Imperial position, so the onslaught on the left came as a surprise, though mist had delayed the early attack that Gustavus had planned.

The delay was crucial, because it enabled Pappenheim to arrive and secure the left of the Imperial position, though almost immediately he was mortally wounded by a cannon-ball. Just as the Swedish position strengthened, the mist thickened once more, so they were unable to pursue their advantage. As the mist fell again Gustavus was killed. Fortunately for the Swedish cause, the court chaplain, Fabricius, led the singing of the psalm 'Sustain us by Thy mighty Word' and the panic in the Swedish ranks was curtailed. Though the Swedes risked defeat, Bernard of Saxe-Weimar, on whom command had fallen, determined to avenge the king's death. As light fell, Saxe-Weimar succeeded in capturing Waldstein's artillery, while Waldstein acted against advice and decided on a tactical withdrawal. The Swedes lost some 6,000 men, approximatley a third of their army through death, injury and desertion; Imperial losses remain something of a mystery because Waldstein left the field, but they are likely to have been about the same or lower, since the Swedes had been assaulting a partially entrenched position. Historians consider the battle inconclusive, but by the military standards of the day (that is, since Waldstein had chosen to leave the field of battle) it was regarded as a Swedish victory. In terms of army size shortly after the battle, the advantage lay distinctly with the Imperial forces, though for Guthrie, its most recent historian, 'Lützen was a defeat for both sides.'

The prestige of Gustavus over his troops was revealed posthumously by the fact that the troops resorted to mutiny shortly after his death to secure their backpay from 1631. In the spring of 1633 the Swedish army settled itself into camp at Donauwörth for three months, in Monro's words, 'resolving to enterprise no exployt or hostility against the Enemy, till such time as they should know, who should content them for their by-past service'. Oxenstierna was forced to buy off the officers with grants of conquered land in lieu of the vast sums owed them. Most richly 'rewarded' of all was Bernard of Saxe-Weimar, who was elevated to the title of Duke of Franconia. The Swedish army had become an army of creditors who had to reimburse themselves from occupied Catholic territory. Surprisingly, in view of the background of discontent, the battle of Hessisch-Oldendorf on 8 July 1633, fought between armies of approximately the same size of about 14,500 men, with the Protestants commanded by Duke George of Brunswick-Lüneburg, was a Protestant victory. Yet after the battle, the Swedish army again mutinied.

Louis XIII, King of France shown here being crowned by victory after the successful siege of La Rochelle, (1628) [Philippe de Champaigne] (1601–43; king from 1610). (AKG, Berlin)

Habsburg family alliance, victory at Nordlingen and French fears of encirclement

After the death of Gustavus Adolphus, it was inevitable that France would increase weight in European affairs. Sweden was weakened by the minority of the new queen, Christina who was six years old when she acceded, and the collective government provided by the Regency lacked cohesion. In contrast, France had a king of age to rule and a chief minister who wished to increase the king's 'reputation' by ensuring that any peace with Spain, regarded as the principal enemy of the Bourbon dynasty, should be 'certain, honourable and one which our allies could see as advantageous'. Historians have debated the respective political roles played by Louis XIII of France and his chief minister, the formidable Armand-Jean du Plessis, Cardinal de Richelieu. Both unquestionably wanted to extend French influence in Europe and break free from what

increasingly seemed like joint Austrian–Spanish–Habsburg 'encirclement'. France appeared the stronger of the two co-guarantors of the Heilbronn League a union of the princes of the Upper and Lower Rhenish, Swabian and Franconian military circles under Swedish and French leadership formed on 23 April 1633. Each of the circles was to contribute 2.5 million *reichsthaler* annually, while the Swedes were given overall military direction of the League forces. The Franco-Swedish Treaty of Bärwalde was renewed, with the subsidies owed Sweden thenceforth to be paid into the treasury of the League rather than that of Sweden. In early September 1634 the Heilbronn League turned over the mighty Rhine fortress of Phillipsburg in return for a promise of French assistance. The French had already gained Ehrenbreitstein and Coblenz in 1632.

The famous triple portrait of Armand-Jean du Plessis, Cardinal de Richelieu (1585–1642), Chief Minister of Louis XIII of France (1624–42). [Philippe de Champaigne] (Ann Ronan Picture Library)

While the Heilbronn League had a new and powerful foreign protector, there was a decisive split in the ranks of the German princes: Saxony refused to join the League, and tried to dissuade the elector of Brandenburg from doing so. Oxenstierna

ABOVE Assassination of Waldstein at Eger, 25 February 1634. (AKG, Berlin)

BELOW Assassination of Waldstein at Eger, 25 February 1634. The initial attack on his headquaters by foreign mercenaries led by Butler, Gordon and Lesley. (AKG, Berlin)

Cardinal-Infante Fernando (1609–41), brother of Philip IV, Spanish commander and governor-general of the Spanish Netherlands. [Velázquez] (Ann Ronan Picture Library)

succeeded in persuading John George of Saxony to join in a spring campaign against the emperor, but the elector insisted on a campaign in Silesia. He also required that this command be given to Count Matthias Thurn, the exiled leader of the Bohemian rebellion. In October 1633, Waldstein attacked Thurn's headquarters at Steinau. Thurn handed over all of the occupied towns of northern Silesia as the price of his freedom. Waldstein then moved forward through Lusatia to the line of the river Oder, and began a campaign against Brandenburg and Saxony. Brandenburg's claim to Pomerania, the essential base of operations for Sweden in Germany, acted as an additional source of dissension in the Protestant alliance. On 23 April 1634, Brandenburg demanded that the Swedes evacuate Pomerania, which they refused to do. Following the elector's lead, neither the Upper nor Lower Saxon circles would join the Heilbronn League, and it remained primarily an organisation of Protestant princes from the south-west. As Guthrie states: 'this area was precisely that most dependent on Swedish protection anyway.'

By the end of 1633, Waldstein was distrusted by everyone, most of all the emperor, who regretted the plenary powers he had granted in the panic after Breitenfeld. On 12 January 1634, Ferdinand II dispatched emissaries to Waldstein's camp at Pilsen, demanding he move his troops into Bavaria. Waldstein reacted by demanding all his officers swear an oath of loyalty to him. Two of the leading commanders, Piccolomini and Gallas, fled the camp then issued an order declaring Waldstein's command to be at an end, which was confirmed by the emperor on 18 February and the army began to desert *en masse*. Finally, on 25 February, a coup masterminded by foreign mercenaries (Butler, Gordon and Lesley) led to the assassination of Waldstein and his immediate supporters at Eger.

With Waldstein dead, Ferdinand, king of Hungary (the future Ferdinand III), was given command of the Imperial forces. His cousin, Ferdinand (Fernando), Cardinal-Infante of Spain, was given command of the Spanish expeditionary force in northern Italy. The two Ferdinands were to join their forces and push west, clearing the 'Spanish Road' between northern Italy and the Low Countries. The king of Hungary joined with the Bavarian troops under Aldringen to recapture Regensburg. They retook it on 22 July 1634, made it their military camp, and pushed west up both banks of the Danube, taking Donauwörth in August, and besieging the city of Nördlingen. Meanwhile, the Swedish forces under the joint command of Gustavus Horn and Bernard of Saxe-Weimar pushed eastward to meet the assault, reaching the vicinity of Nördlingen on 23 August.

The Swedes were badly outnumbered. The Protestant forces numbered some 22,000 to 24,000 men including many who were raw recruits, while the Catholic allies could muster some 33,000 to 36,000 men, many of whom were battle-hardened troops. After an unsuccessful assault on the trenches on 5 September, on the 6th the Swedes attacked the prepared positions of the combined forces (See map on p.58). After a series of failed assaults against the hilltop on which the Spanish were entrenched, Gustav Horn's forces retreated behind Bernard of Saxe-Weimar's line. Just at that moment, the Imperial cavalry attacked. Saxe-Weimar's line was broken and the Swedish army dissolved in chaos. By the end of the day, the Swedish field army had virtually ceased to exist. All its 68 cannon had been captured, along with 300 standards, nearly treble the number the Imperial forces had lost at Breitenfeld. Eight thousand men were dead and 4,000 captured against relatively light casualties among the Catholic allies – 1,500 dead and 2,000 wounded. Horn was captured and Saxe-Weimar was forced to flee westward, calling his garrisons to join him, hoping to make a stand, if at all, at the Rhine.

The battle of Lützen, 16 November 1632

1. Gustavus' attack.
2. Brahe's attack.
3. Bernard's attack.

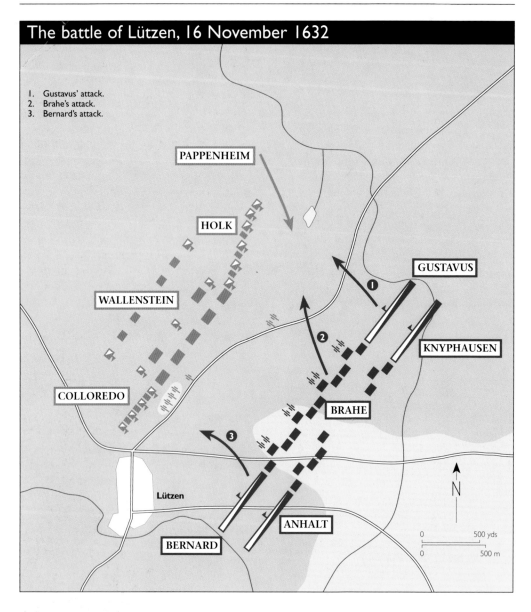

The Heilbronn League – which was to have been the bulwark of the Protestant cause – was reduced to a band of landless refugees. After Nördlingen, Franconia, Swabia and Württemberg fell to the Spanish and Imperial forces almost without a shot fired, Charles, Duke of Lorraine and Johann von Werth threatened the French positions in Lorraine. To meet this threat, La Force pulled back his troops, leaving the Rhineland dangerously exposed. The Imperialists were swift to take advantage of this weakness. On 24 January 1635 they took Philippsburg, and Speyer followed on 2 February. On 22 February, the remaining French forces withdrew to the left bank of the Rhine, followed swiftly by Bernard of Saxe-Weimar's troops. Franco-Swedish forces were able to recover Speyer on 21 March, but they remained confined to the left bank of the Rhine.

John George of Saxony, having never been a willing opponent of the emperor, had negotiated with Ferdinand II even when his armies invaded Bohemia in the summer of 1634. The negotiations produced a tentative arrangement; the Preliminaries of Pirna,

agreed on 24 November. Resumed on 2 April 1635 the negotiations resulted in the Peace of Prague on 30 May. The Peace was open to almost any ruler who cared to sign up to its terms and who would, in return, receive an amnesty and restoration of any expropriated titles and lands. The sole exceptions were princes in arms against the emperor prior to Gustavus Adolphus' invasion of 1630. When the elector of Brandenburg joined the Peace, he managed to extract a concession from the emperor that any peace made with Sweden would recognise his expectancy of the Pomeranian inheritance. This guaranteed that the war would continue since, except as a consequence of military disaster, Sweden would never give up her bulwark on the southern Baltic shore.

ABOVE John George, elector of Saxony, 1585–1656, (elector from 1611). (AKG, Berlin)

BELOW Louis XIII leading the French army for the relief of Corbie in 1636. (Roger-Viollet)

The Franco-Swedish war in Germany

Phase One: to the death of Banér, 1635–41

Meanwhile, a *casus belli* for war between France and Spain had presented itself. Phillip-Christopher von Sötern, Elector of Trier and Bishop of Speyer, had placed himself under French protection early in 1632. As the situation in the Rhineland grew more chaotic, Spanish forces stationed in Luxembourg decided to strike out at this French ally. On 26 March 1635, the Spaniards captured both Trier and its elector. Such an attack on a prince under French protection could not go unanswered and France declared war on Spain on 26 May.

In the first year of French intervention, the Imperial army took Kaiserslautern and Heidelberg and besieged Mainz. By December, Mainz too, was in Imperial hands. Richelieu was shaken by the failure of French arms. He appreciated that the safety of the Rhine defence line, and thus northern France, depended on the experienced troops of Saxe-Weimar. For his part, Bernard realised that no further help was to be expected from the German Protestant princes, virtually all of whom had joined the Peace of Prague, and began to negotiate with France. On 19 November he agreed that, in return for annual subsidies of a million *livres*, he would maintain an army of 12,000 infantry and 6,000 cavalry. Saxe-Weimar was promised the Landgravate of Alsace, and rights over all lands conquered by him. The Swedes were irate that their French allies had 'debauched' an army sworn to Swedish service but were powerless to do anything about it.

If 1635 was a bad year for French armies 1636, with the exception of the campaign in Upper Alsace, was worse. On the advice of Maximilian of Bavaria, Spain determined on a fast-moving invasion of France through Picardy and Franche-Comté. The Cardinal-Infante, having borrowed Johann von Werth's cavalry from the emperor, entered Picardy and, in Turner's words, destroyed 'a

great deal' of it and 'burnt many villages'. The Spaniards advanced as far as Corbie, some 80 miles from Paris. This fortress and two others were betrayed to the Spanish. Meanwhile, Charles, Duke of Lorraine and Gallas advanced into Burgundy from Franche-Comté, besieged Dôle and reached Dijon. Paris was filled with panic and the fall of Richelieu was expected daily. In the end, Louis XIII rallied enough troops to drive the lightly -armed invaders from Picardy. Gallas' advance was halted by a stubborn garrison of St -Jean-de-Losne. The invasion melted away, but there is little doubt that the crisis would have been rendered even more serious had Spain been successful in mounting a third invasion, from the south, a year earlier. In the event the invasion of Languedoc in 1637, which resulted in the siege of Lecuate, was a damp squib.

In the winter of 1637–38 Bernard of Saxe-Weimar made himself master of the Forest Towns of the Rhine, most notably Rhinefelden. There, he fought two bloody battles, losing the first, which allowed the Imperial forces to reinforce the city. He won the second in March, capturing the opposing commander, the feared cavalry general, Johann von Werth. It was not until May 1638, after he had received French reinforcements under de Guébriant, that Saxe-Weimar was in a position to exploit his victory at Rheinfelden by moving against the key fortress of Breisach. Situated on a promontory above the Rhine, the great fortress was the key to control of the Habsburg lands scattered along the Rhine. Saxe-Weimar withdrew after a first siege in June 1638. In August, having received further French reinforcements commanded by the young Turenne, Saxe-Weimar returned to his task. After defeating Imperial forces at Wittenweier on 18 August, Saxe-Weimar encircled what was considered the impregnable Breisach and prepared to starve out its defenders. The garrison, Sir James Turner considered, was the 'epitome of the miseries of Samaria and Jerusalem in the Holy Land and of Sancerre and [La Rochelle] in France'. Finally, on

17 December, Breisach's governor, von Rheinach, capitulated and was granted honourable terms. These were nearly revoked when Saxe-Weimar discovered that some of his men held prisoner in the fortress had been driven by starvation to eat their dead comrades. Initially the fruits of victory proved elusive to Louis XIII, since Saxe-Weimar fell into dispute with the French government. After the death of Bernard of Saxe-Weimar on 11 July 1639, d'Erlach, his astute second-in-command, began to negotiate with potential paymasters. The Swedes were interested, as was Karl-Ludwig of the Palatinate. Even the emperor was interested in buying out one of his enemies, but in October d'Erlach and his commanders determined to serve the king of France.

After the conclusion of the Suedo-Polish Truce of Stuhmsdorf in September 1635, the Swedish army under Torstennson which had been garrisoning Poland could be transferred to Germany, where there was a pressing need for reinforcements. Banér's Swedish troops had retreated from Bohemia and taken up quarters in the bishopric of Magdeburg. The army was unpaid, mutinous and plagued by desertion. On 16 October, Saxony formally declared war on Sweden. The Saxons and their new Imperial allies moved down the river Elbe to intercept the disorganised Swedish troops. Another force in the north sought, but failed, to prevent Torstennson's army from meeting up with Banér's troops in the bastion of Mecklenburg and Pomerania.

On 10 July 1636, Johan Banér had no more than 14,090 troops at his disposition, yet in September he took to the offensive again. He moved from his camp at Werben down the Elbe towards Naumberg. A joint Saxon–Imperial force moved to intercept the Swedes, whom they met at Wittstock in Brandenburg. On 4 October, the Swedes inflicted a crushing defeat on their more numerous foes. (See map on p.59). Banér's Swedish army of only 16,378 men (a force of 3,500 men was under his direct command with Torstennson as second-in-command; 4,736 men were held in reserve, while the remainder were commanded by the mercenary Scots colonel James king) found itself in an inferior strategic position to the opposing Saxon and Imperial army of about 19,000 men, which was on a hilltop and had the advantage of covering woodland. The main Swedish force of 5,242 men under Leslie attempted to storm the heights, but the route was so steep that it rapidly found itself in difficulty; casualties were high, the cannon was lost and the Imperial forces sounded victory. Yet Banér had earlier divided his forces, and the left wing of 2,900 men led by James King and the Swede Torston Stålhandske persevered in an outflanking manoeuvre behind woodland, which resulted in the capture of the Saxon cannon, according to Montecuccoli, without having fired a shot since 'the cannoneers had run away'. The Imperial cavalry managed to escape, but the losses of the infantry were substantial. Though it has been argued that Banér's tactics were 'unique in the military history of the period', Wittstock was a case of superior resolution bringing about the decisive victory, which rescued the Swedish position in Germany and preserved its vital base of Mecklenburg and Pomerania. Yet the result was achieved at a high cost, with perhaps a third of the Swedish forces killed or wounded as against losses of up to 60 per cent on the side of the Imperialists and Saxons. Turner criticised the insufficiency of the Swedish reserve at Wittstock and contended that Banér 'had been undoubtedly beaten if the battle and left wing had not prevail'd'. The Imperial commander, Montecuccoli, contested the verdict that it was a clear Swedish victory at nightfall: 'the number of dead, both officers and men, and captured flags and standards was equal on both sides.' However, the Imperialist and Saxon forces chose to withdraw; had they instead chosen to attack early the following day, 'they might well have been able to defeat the Swedes who were just as apprehensive, had suffered just as much damage, and had not benefited at all from the captured cannon.'

The first battle of Nordligen, 6 September 1634

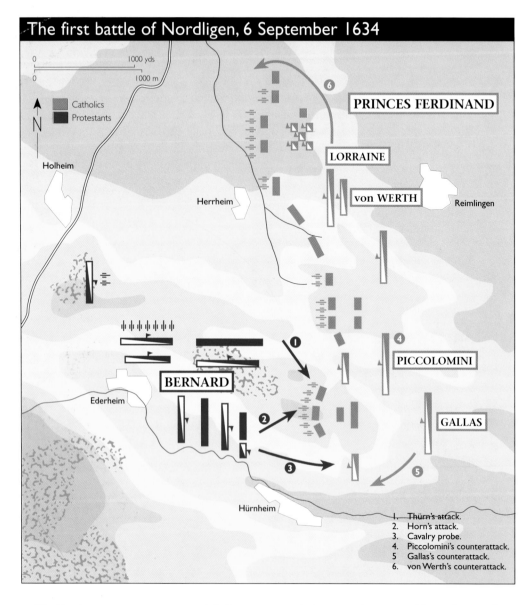

0 ————— 1000 yds
0 ————— 1000 m

N

■ Catholics
■ Protestants

Holheim

Herrheim

PRINCES FERDINAND

LORRAINE

von WERTH   Reimlingen

BERNARD

Ederheim

PICCOLOMINI

GALLAS

Hürnheim

1. Thürn's attack.
2. Horn's attack.
3. Cavalry probe.
4. Piccolomini's counterattack.
5. Gallas's counterattack.
6. von Werth's counterattack.

The Swedes were once more out of their Baltic redoubt. Banér dispatched Wrangel against George William of Brandenburg in an effort to overawe him into an alliance, as Gustavus Adolphus had done five years before. The effort failed, and George William drew closer to the emperor and began to raise an army of his own. Banér and the Swedes moved south into Saxony, besieging Leipzig. The siege failed, and in January 1637 Banér and Leslie fell back on Torgau. Their depleted army was badly overextended, and was outnumbered 2:1 by the Imperial army under Gallas. By a clever tactical retreat, they were able to elude Gallas and escape to the Baltic coast; although a third of the army was lost to famine and disease. By the end of 1637 the Swedes clung with difficulty to pockets of Pomerania.

Chancellor Oxenstierna wished to negotiate a separate peace with the Ferdinand II and to extract Sweden from the German quagmire. He played for time, negotiating one treaty after another with Richelieu and ratifying none of them. It was not until March 1638 that the prolonged negotiations finally produced the Treaty of

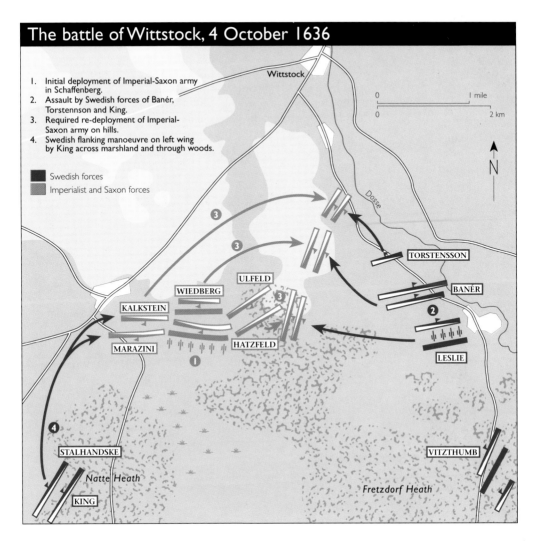

The battle of Wittstock, 4 October 1636

1. Initial deployment of Imperial-Saxon army in Schaffenberg.
2. Assault by Swedish forces of Banér, Torstennson and King.
3. Required re-deployment of Imperial-Saxon army on hills.
4. Swedish flanking manoeuvre on left wing by King across marshland and through woods.

Swedish forces
Imperialist and Saxon forces

Wittstock

0 ___ 1 mile
0 ___ 2 km

N

Dosse

TORSTENSSON
BANÉR
ULFELD
WIEDBERG
KALKSTEIN
MARAZINI   HATZFELD
LESLIE
STALHANDSKE   VITZTHUMB
Natte Heath   Fretzdorf Heath
KING

Hamburg. Each side agreed that during the three-year term of the treaty no separate peace with the emperor would be concluded. The French were to pay the Swedes an annual subsidy of one million *livres*. In return, the Swedes were to carry the war into the Habsburg dominions in the east, while the French army would continue to fight in the Rhineland. After concluding the Treaty of Hamburg with France, Oxenstierna was in possession of French subsidies; he also sent Banér 14,000 fresh recruits from Sweden. In July 1638, Banér was in a position to go on the offensive, and cleared Mecklenburg and Pomerania of Imperial troops. He then drove the Imperial forces under Gallas back into Silesia and Bohemia.

In January 1639 Banér swung west through the Brunswick duchies; then he turned east against the Saxons and their Imperial allies. The Swedes drove the Saxons back to Dresden. At Chemnitz in Saxony, they met the Imperial army under Archduke Leopold-William, Ferdinand III's brother. On 14 April 1639, they inflicted a crushing defeat on the archduke, opening the road into Silesia and Bohemia. Banér continued east, taking Pirna and destroying another Imperial army near Brandeis. By May 1639, he was encamped before the walls of Prague, but he was unable to sustain the siege; he eventually withdrew to the Elbe. In December 1640 the armies of Sweden, France and Brunswick assembled at Erfurt for a combined campaign. The combined offensive accomplished nothing. The allied forces penetrated as far south as the Danube at Regensburg and in January 1641, they briefly invested the city, but the Danube thawed and the half-hearted siege was lifted. The allied forces split up and retired to their bases.

Phase Two: Torstennson and Wrangel, 1641–48

Banér's army, whose discipline had always been suspect, mutinied on his death on 20 May 1641. Oxenstierna appointed Torstennson, general of artillery under Gustavus Adolphus, as commander of the Swedish forces. In the interim, the armies were to be under the control of Wrangel. Torstennson arrived in November 1641 with 7,000 fresh recruits and quelled the mutinies. He went on the offensive in the spring of 1642. Striking east, he defeated the elector of Saxony's forces at Schweidnitz. With the road into the Imperial lands thus opened, he moved south-east into Moravia, taking the capital Olomuoc (Olmütz) in June 1642. Torstennson fortified Olomuoc, which served as the linchpin of Swedish- held territory in the east for the remainder of the war, though during this time its population fell from 30,000 to 2,000. With Vienna threatened, the emperor assembled a large force under Piccolomini and Archduke Leopold-William. Torstennson (See map on p.62) fell back through Silesia and besieged Leipzig in Saxony. On 2 November 1642, the Imperial forces caught up with the Swedes. Torstennson was outnumbered and fell back on Breitenfeld. While the Imperial forces were assembling their ranks, Torstennson led his army against their left, charged through a deadly cannonade, broke the Imperial lines and engulfed the remainder of the Habsburg army. In this second battle of Breitenfeld, the Imperialists lost 5,000 killed, and 5,000 captured, while the Swedish losses were 2,000 killed and 2,000 seriously wounded. Leipzig fell within the month.

The French victory at Rocroi on 19 May 1643, the first victory of Louis de Bourbon,

prince of Condé who after 1647 was known as the 'great Condé, reinforced the French preoccupation with the Low Countries front. Condé had surprised the Spanish commander Melos with a superior force of some 23,000 men; there were only 18,000 Spanish infantry and a small cavalry force. The Spanish had more cannon and made effective use of them on 18 May; but the following day, Condé isolated the Spanish infantry force, inflicting enormous damage on it: 8,000 were killed and nearly 7,000 were taken prisoner. The French captured 60 standards and lost some 2,000 dead.

It was not until October 1643 that de Guébriant finally received sufficient reinforcements to return to the offensive in Germany. The Bavarian army under von Werth, together with reinforcements from the emperor and Charles Duke of Lorraine, responded swiftly to the threat to their winter quarters in Swabia. At Tuttlingen on 24 November 1643, the Lorraine and Imperial forces commanded by Charles of Lorraine and von Werth crushed the French and Weimar forces commanded by de Guébriant with an attacking force of only 18,000 men. Fatally wounded, de Guébriant retired to Rottweil, which was besieged by Lorraine's forces. Many of the French forces fled the battle and died of hunger and cold on their retreat. The French lost 4,000 dead and 7,000 taken prisoner at the battle and subsequent engagements and sieges. Tuttlingen demonstrates that a crushing victory could be gained by relatively small forces.

In the wake of the Tuttlingen disaster, Turenne was recalled from the Italian front and placed in command of the French army of Germany. The diversion of Torstennson and the Swedish army into a pre-emptive strike against Denmark had weakened and isolated the French position in Germany. Maximilian of Bavaria was not slow to seize the opportunity. He importuned Ferdinand III for support, and was granted a corps under

Louis II de Bourbon duc d'Enghien and prince of Condé (1621–86). He was a successful commander in 1643 and 1648. (Roger-Viollet)

Second battle of Breitenfeld, 1642

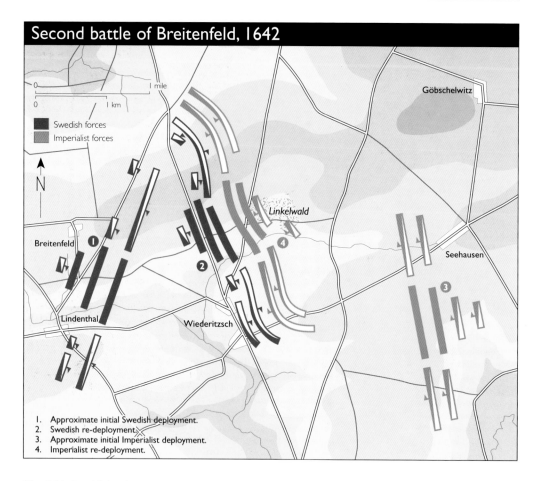

0 _____ 1 mile
0 _____ 1 km

Swedish forces
Imperialist forces

N

Göbschelwitz

Linkelwald

Breitenfeld ①

②

④

Seehausen

③

Lindenthal

Wiederitzsch

1. Approximate initial Swedish deployment.
2. Swedish re-deployment.
3. Approximate initial Imperialist deployment.
4. Imperialist re-deployment.

Hatzfeld. On 15 April 1644, Maximilian sent his forces under von Mercy across the Black Forest toward Turenne. Von Mercy first besieged and, on 11 May 1644, took Überlingen on Lake Constance. On 26 June, von Mercy appeared before Freiburg-im-Breisgau in numbers Turenne could not match; the city fell to the siege on 28 July. Reinforcements under Condé, dispatched by Mazarin in the hopes of saving Freiburg, arrived days too late. The Bavarians were well entrenched in the mountains around Freiburg. Nonetheless, Condé, who had assumed command, determined to make a frontal assault on 3 August and 5 August 1644, but the outcome was unclear. It was a series of bloody encounters rather than a straightforward battle. Each side lost roughly half its army – perhaps 7,500 men on each side – and each remained in the field. Freiburg remained in Bavarian hands; in the event the

Bavarian inferiority in cavalry was decisive, forcing von Mercy to withdraw his army closer to his Bavarian bases. During the retreat he was harassed by the superior French cavalry, which captured his baggage train.

The main French army moved down the Rhine into the Lower Palatinate, taking all of its strong places with the exception of Frankenthal. It then captured Philippsburg and Mainz, each of which was defended by garrisons of only 600 men. The capture of Philippsburg on 9 September 1644 was the first great French advance in the German war since Bernard of Saxe-Weimar's capture of Breisach six years earlier. The French rapidly improved the fortifications, making so bold as to claim that Philippsburg was 'the Casale of Germany' (Casale was the French fortified 'gateway' into Italy). The enormous strategic advantage its possession conferred was to enable subsequent French

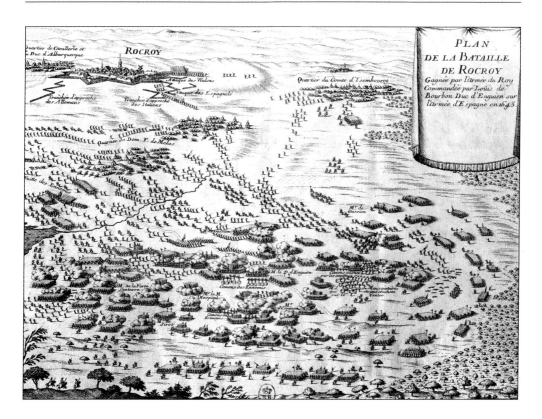

Plan of the battle of Rocroi between France and Spain (19 May 1643) by Charles Sevin, marquis de Quincy. (Roger-Viollet)

invasions of Germany to begin further down the Rhine, thus avoiding the obstacle posed by the Black Forest.

In early 1645, Torstennson was intent on recovering the parts of Bohemia and Moravia lost to the Imperialists during the Danish Intervention. Pushing past the Imperial forces, the Swedes advanced from Eger, through Budweis and Pilsen toward Tabor in Moravia. The emperor had raised such troops as he could and called upon Maximilian of Bavaria for assistance. The combined armies under General Götz pursued Torstennson, catching him at Jankow near Tabor. On 6 March 1645, battle was joined. (See map on p.66-67) The forces were nearly evenly matched, with about 15,000 men each, and the battle was hard fought. The Swedish forces moved through woodland and managed to capture the heights above the Imperial forces and moved their artillery up to this position. The Imperial cavalry met murderous fire from Torstennson's artillery, mounted on the hilltop, and was surrounded by the counter attack of the Swedish cavalry.

A Swedish historian, Åberg, calls Jankow 'a triumph for Torstennson's military genius. For the first time in Swedish history the issue of a battle was decided by the gunners.' The Imperialists received a crushing defeat, losing half their forces with General Götz dead on the field.

Vienna lay open to the conquering Swedes, whose armies, at the end of April 1645, approached within 30 miles of the Austrian capital. Ferdinand III hurriedly fled to Graz. However, rather than pursuing his attack on Vienna, Torstennson determined to secure Moravia by the conquest of the city of Brno (Brünn). The place resisted valiantly for more than five months, giving the Imperial forces in Austria time to regroup. On 31 August 1645, John George of Saxony entered a six-month armistice with the Swedes under the terms of which they were to have right of free passage through the electorate, as well as support in kind and in cash. This armistice was renewed on 14 April 1646 by the Peace of Eilenberg, which remained in effect until the end of the war. Saxony's inglorious role in the Thirty Years' War was at an end.

The Swedish military ascendancy on the eastern front was not replicated in the west. Turenne, hoping to join up with the Swedish forces in Germany, marched through Württemberg but on 2 May 1645 encountered a surprise attack from von Mercy's Bavarian army at the battle of Marienthal (Mergentheim). Turenne lost all his infantry and most of his cavalry: his army of 10,000 was reduced to a fleeing column of 1,500 cavalry. Pursued by the victorious von Mercy, Turenne fell back on Hesse-Cassel. Cardinal Mazarin sent Condé with new forces to rescue the French position. Their united forces encountered the Bavarians in the second battle of Nördlingen (Allerheim) on 3 August and in a desperate and costly struggle, in which von Mercy was killed, the Bavarians were driven back. Von Werth's cavalry had charged down from the hill on the Bavarian left flank, defeated the French right flank but then plundered the French baggage train rather than turning against the French left flank. Turenne reversed the situation by charging and breaking the Bavarian right flank. The Bavarians withdrew the next day, Nordlingen was occupied by the French, and Condé and Turenne reached the Danube, but only after suffering such grievous losses in infantry that they were forced to return to the Rhineland. The French army was not strong enough to besiege Heilbronn in September 1645, while in October a joint Imperial–Bavarian force began recapturing the French gains of earlier in the year.

Reviewing the results of the 1645 campaign, Torstennson concluded that the allies had been defeated by superior co-operation on the part of the Habsburg and Bavarian armies. His plan was that the French and Swedish armies should link up the following year, and advance on a single front, thus preventing either of them from

Cardinal Jules Mazarin (1602–61), Chief Minister of Louis XIV of France (1643–61). [Philippe de Champaigne] (Roger-Viollet)

being attacked by two enemy armies acting in unison. Mazarin was nervous at this suggestion – preferring to use Turenne's army to apply pressure on Spain – and fearful lest the control of military strategy came to rest with the stronger Swedish army. However, Turenne was a hawk who wished to crush the emperor decisively and as a Calvinist he shared little of Mazarin's wish to spare Bavaria. He strongly favoured a military junction with Sweden. He crossed the Rhine at Wesel with perhaps 8,000 men and on 10 August 1646, near Giessen, achieved his intended junction with the much stronger Swedish army under Wrangel. The joint army attacked the Bavarian–Imperial army under Archduke Leopold-William on 14 August and within two days achieved a pincer movement, which cut off its communications and retreat to the south. The archduke was forced to march north, leaving Bavaria virtually undefended: 'We can go right into Bavaria without resistance and spread terror everywhere,' wrote one French officer to Mazarin. The reason was that the Bavarian fortresses had tiny garrisons of fewer than 300 men: they were too weak to withstand a siege and surrendered at the sight of a victorious invader. Maximilian of Bavaria learnt of the allied breakthrough on 19 August and was forced to flee Munich. He opened negotiations with the French and, by the Treaty of Ulm (14 March 1647) abandoned his alliance with Ferdinand III.

Bavaria had made its peace and, though the peace only lasted until September, the French and Swedes should have had things their own way within the empire in 1647. This was not to be the case. The reason was the slackening of the Dutch war effort against Spain. This placed greater importance on the French military effort in the Low Countries, while allowing the Spaniards to shift their forces to the southern frontiers of the Low Countries and

Jankow: Initial dispositions

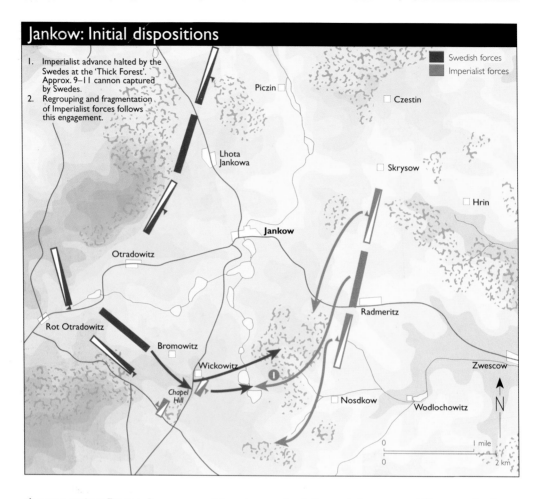

1. Imperialist advance halted by the Swedes at the 'Thick Forest'. Approx. 9–11 cannon captured by Swedes.
2. Regrouping and fragmentation of Imperialist forces follows this engagement.

Swedish forces
Imperialist forces

Piczin
Czestin
Lhota Jankowa
Skrysow
Hrin
Jankow
Otradowitz
Radmeritz
Rot Otradowitz
Bromowitz
Zwescow
Wickowitz
Chapel Hill
Nosdkow
Wodlochowitz

N

0   1 mile
0   2 km

the war against France. In response, Mazarin ordered Turenne to move his forces into northern France. The Weimarian troops, proud successors of Bernard of Saxe-Weimar's army, refused to serve beyond the German frontiers. The Swedes shifted their point of attack eastward after taking Nördlingen in April 1647. The Swedish forces under Wrangel besieged the city of Eger in northern Bohemia. Despite the intervention of the Imperial army, it fell in July 1647. The Swedes moved forward, although a portion of their forces were destroyed by von Werth's surprise attack at Triebel on 25 August. In September 1647 Maximilian of Bavaria shifted alliance and entered into the Treaty of Pilsen with Ferdinand III. The Bavarian army moved through the Upper Palatinate and reinforced the Imperial troops in Bohemia. Wrangel fell

back through Saxony and Hesse to the far side of the river Weser.

What was to prove the last campaigning season of the war opened in March 1648 with Turenne and Wrangel uniting their forces at Ansbach for an attack against Bavaria. Their united forces moved south, pushing the Imperial and Bavarian armies across the Danube. The opposing armies finally met at Zusmarhausen near Augsburg. There, on 17 May 1648, the last of the Imperial field armies was defeated, its commander killed and his army routed. After Zusmarhausen, the remaining Imperial and Bavarian forces fell back, first to Augsburg and then beyond the river Inn. Piccolomini was recalled from Spanish service and placed in command of the remaining Imperial forces. He managed to hold the Swedes behind the river Inn,

Jankow: Phase two

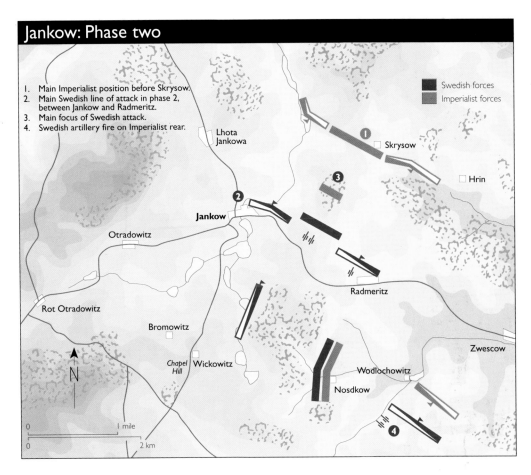

1. Main Imperialist position before Skrysow.
2. Main Swedish line of attack in phase 2, between Jankow and Radmeritz.
3. Main focus of Swedish attack.
4. Swedish artillery fire on Imperialist rear.

Swedish forces
Imperialist forces

Lhota Jankowa
Skrysow
Hrin
Jankow
Otradowitz
Radmeritz
Rot Otradowitz
Bromowitz
Zwescow
Chapel Hill | Wickowitz
Wodlochowitz
Nosdkow
N
0   1 mile
0   2 km

although all Bavaria behind that line was devastated with a fury notable even for that age. The Swedes withdrew beyond the Lech, pursued by Piccolomini. In November 1648, news reached the armies in Bavaria that peace had been declared.

Prior to invading Bavaria, Wrangel had dispatched a small column under Königsmarck to invade Bohemia once more. Passing through the Upper Palatinate into Bohemia,

destroying all in his path, Königsmarck appeared before the walls of Prague on 26 July 1648. He was able to enter one quarter of the city which was betrayed to him by a former Imperial officer. Despite possession of a portion of the city, and the arrival of reinforcements, the Swedes were unable to take the remainder of the town. The stalemate was ended only by the arrival of news of the conclusion of the Peace of Westphalia.

The Mercenaries

Colonel Robert Monro (c.1590–1680) commanded a Scots mercenary regiment called Mackay's regiment, and later Monro's during the Thirty Years' War. Mercenaries were a typical feature of the war, and we know more about Monro than others because he left his memoirs, which are in essence a regimental and social history. He considered that an army career offered the possibility of achieving one's potential through hard work, diligence and ability. It was far better to 'live honourably abroad, and with credit, then to encroach (as many do) on their friends at home'. For Monro, the profession of arms was 'a calling', and his service in the German conflict was in part for his 'better instruction', and in part a matter of principle, supporting as he did the Bohemian and Protestant cause. He was wounded three times, at Oldenburg in 1627, at the siege of Stralsund in 1628 and at Nuremberg in 1632.

Monro was a Presbyterian whose military service in the Thirty Years' War was given to successive Lutheran monarchs, first Christian IV of Denmark, then Gustavus Adolphus of Sweden, fighting against the Roman Catholic emperor. Proud of both his nationality and religion, he attributed victory over the Catholic Imperial forces at Breitenfeld largely to 'the invincible Scots, whose prayers to God were more effectuall through Christ, then theirs through the intercession of Saints'. Unlike many mercenaries, Monro based his choice of side firmly on religious principle and opposition to 'Catholique Potentates' who would overthrow 'our estates at home' and 'make shipwracke of our consciences' by 'leading us unto Idolatry'. Gustavus Adolphus' example of 'Piety and religious exercise' was particularly commended by Monro: 'as His Majesty was religious himselfe, so he

maintained good lawes and good discipline, grounded on religion and holiness of life.' The king sought to employ both Lutherans and Calvinists, and thus to heal the rift within the evangelical cause. Monro was much impressed by Gustavus' speech to his troops, in which the Swedish king:

'was perswaded, that though God should call him out of the world, yet the Lord would not abandon his owne Cause … he had no other intention in prosecuting these warres, but onely to pull downe the tyranny of the house of Austria; and to obtain a solid and settled peace unto all men, that were interested in the quarrell. For Monro, it was Gustavus '… *and none other under God, who helped them [the Germans] to their liberties, He it was and none other releeved Israell'.*

That, at least, was Monro's understanding of the politics of the war, but it was a particular understanding, and it was not necessarily shared even by recruits from the British Isles. Another mercenary, Sydnam Poyntz, changed both sides and religion but did not specifically match the two, enlisting with Protestant Saxony soon after his own conversion to Catholicism. Poyntz rose to the rank of captain in the Saxon army, but when taken prisoner by the Imperialists he 'lost againe all that I had'. Making the best of his circumstances, he changed sides, and finding favour with his capturer, Colonel Butler – the principal murderer of Waldstein– he was able to rebuild his career and finances and 'send home often tymes Mony to my Wife, who its seemes spent at home what I got abroad'. In general terms, as Dr Geoffrey

French commander turned: Henri II d'Orléans, duc de Longuevelle (1595–1663) [*Man on Horseback*, by Gerard ter Borch, 1617–81] c.1646–47. (AKG, Berlin)

Henri de la Tour d'Auvergne, Vicomte de Turenne, French commander in Germany (1611–75). (AKG, Berlin)

Mortimer expresses it: 'whether nominally Protestant or Catholic, the armies themselves were as religiously as they were ethnically cosmopolitan, embracing men of all religions or none so long as they would serve'. Monro was as keen to have the potentially Catholic Irish join his forces as the English and Scots.

In Poyntz's case, career and profit came before conviction, but with Monro, the career of arms was also the progress of the soldier of Jesus Christ. It was the duty of the Christian soldier to 'walke in his wayes without wearying' and to bear his own cross and suffer misery in patience. His duty was to prepare for death 'by unfained repentance, thinking more often of death than of long life, call[ing] to minde Gods judgements, and the pains of Hell' so that his conscience was clear and he had no reason to fear death. Monro, on the other hand, was aware that mercenaries did not

necessarily display the same degree of 'vertue' that he advocated. He criticised the 'crueltie and inhumanitie' of Tilly's Catholic League army and condemned the immoderate conduct of Pappenheim's forces after the failure at Maastricht. Looting was allowable to the Swedish army in occupied Bavaria, but burnings were unauthorised acts of revenge by soldiers. Hostages were taken, but as a guarantee of payment of contributions.

The difference between success and failure on the battlefield was critical in securing contributions: 'the Townes of Germanie are best friends ever to the masters of the field, in flattering the victorious, and in persecuting of the loser.' Good commanders, such as Banér, were those who gave their troops 'some liberty of booty: to the end that they might prove the more resolute another time, for Souldiers will not refuse to undergoe any hazard, when they see their Officers willing to reward them with honour and profit'. Sometimes, as at Breitenfeld, supposed friends, the Saxons, were as acquisitive as foes: 'they made booty of our wagons and goods, too good a recompence for Cullions that had left their Duke, betrayed their country and the good cause.'

Gustavus Adolphus was specially praised for ensuring that his armies did not 'oppresse the poore, which made them cry for a blessing to his Majesty and his Army' and his willingness to expand the size of his forces by recruiting prisoners, as after Breitenfeld. The encouragement of desertion in the opposing army was a deliberate tactic. The securing of food supplies was critical to Gustavus, 'knowing well how hungry men could be contented with little, in time of need'. For Monro, hunger was the great enemy, 'for oftimes an Army is lost sooner by hunger than by fighting ... For to hunger, and to fight valiantly, doth not agree with nature ... Armes doe resist Armes, but to resist hunger, no Fort, no Strength, no Moate or Fossie is able to do it.' Service under Christian IV was made more palatable by good quarters and good wine and beer, while

Gustavus Adolphus in der Schlact bei Lutzen, 1632.
(Herzog Anton Ulrich Museum)

the march from Würzburg to Frankfurt in 1631 'being profitable as it was pleasant to the eye, we see that Souldiers have not always so hard a life, as the common opinion is'. Yet soldiers also needed their pay: on another occasion, Monro records that '... we were all of us discontented; being too much toyled with marching, working and watching, without any pay or gaines for honest men.' Von Mansfeld was a notoriously bad paymaster: Poyntz recalls that he and his comrades had 'nothing from our Generall but what we got by pillage which as the Proverb is lightly come as lightly goes'. Mutiny was inevitable, as was the case with Swedish troops at Donauwörth for three months in the spring of 1633, when the army commanders rewarded themselves but did not pay the troops their year's back pay. Some mutinies, such as those of the Dutch ('not the best Souldiers in extremitie of danger') were a cover to avoid danger, however, and no more than 'a Cloake of discontentment'.

Impact of war

Recording events

What did a soldier do if he was forced to take early retirement? Few military engravers of the 17th century could lay claim to quite such a dramatic start to their career as battlefield artists in the service of the king of France as Sébastien de Pontaut, seigneur de Beaulieu, who lost his right arm in the siege of Philippsburg, a key fortress on the Rhine, in 1644. Regrettably, it may also explain why other engravers were more talented than he. Their works illustrate that combination of propaganda, military reporting and artistic endeavour which gives the largely forgotten career of the military engraver its importance in the 17th century. The engravings of the first military engagements of the war had been relatively crude endeavours. One has only to view the images of von Mansfeld's siege of Pilsen, or John George of Saxony's capture of Bautzen, to see that military engraving was a poorly established servant of the victor powers, and subsequent military historians, at the outset of the Thirty Years' War.

All this changed with the advent of the Swiss engraver Matthäus Merian the elder who died in 1650. Best known for his later topographical engravings of some 450 German and Austrian cities, Merian applied himself to the needs of military reporting with considerable talent. We cannot know how reliable his work was, and the extent to which he used employees to produce first sketches which he then reworked as the finished article; what is clear is that by the time of Gustavus Adolphus' invasion of Germany in 1630 there was a real talent capable of reporting the great battles of Breitenfeld and Lützen, and no military account of these battles is complete without reference to the visual image. Merian's images were skilfully marketed in Abelin's *Theatrum Europaeum*, the format of which

imposed its own limitations: significant battlefield engagements had on occasion to be split into two or three images, the relationship between them sometimes being lost unless another, separate, full-scale version of the battle survives.

Two other features of the German style of military engraving pioneered by Merian are also important to note. The first is the accuracy of the detail of the depictions. By the last year of the war, with the siege of Prague, the engravings could depict the details of the storming of a breach with the accuracy almost of a modern photograph. The second feature was a concern for topographical accuracy of the terrain of battle (this is scarcely surprising given Merian's interest in city topography) but it is a particularly telling aspect of some of the later engravings. Merian's depiction of the battle of Jankow in 1645 sets the military action against the terrain much in the way that would a modern battlefield plan. Italian influences were also brought into play in the entourage of Montecuccoli, but there is little evidence of any greater originality in the Italian battlefield depictions.

The effect of war on the civilian population

One of the features of modern warfare is that it heavily involves the civilian population; indeed, the number of civilian casualties tends to exceed those of the military. In this respect, the Thirty Years' War had some of the features of modern warfare. It is believed that the sack of Magdeburg in May 1631 – the single worst atrocity of the war – resulted in the death of some 24,000 people with many more killed by the resulting fire than by the military action. The German conflict brought civilians into regular contact with warfare and the military on a scale never seen before for three reasons. Firstly, because of the duration of the conflict. Not all areas of Germany were affected by the war all the time: as has been seen, southern Germany was largely spared from the conflict before 1631. Nevertheless, Germany had never before been the battleground for other European powers for more than a few years at a time. The war was always remembered subsequently because of its longevity. Secondly, because of the scale of the conflict. Armies were rarely as large as their commanders intended them to be, because of difficulties in recruitment and the problem of large-scale desertion: but by the 1630s large armies were operating in the German theatre of war on a regular basis. These larger armies required levels of recruitment and logistical support on a scale that was much greater than in earlier conflicts. The third reason was in the nature of warfare itself. War, in Gustavus Adolphus' phrase, was supposed to 'sustain war', that is to say, armies had to be mobile or else they starved. Once the recruitment cost of the army had been met, the operating costs fell largely on the civilian population by means of three mechanisms: accord terms for the surrender of towns; war booty, which was taken illegitimately by the troops; and 'contributions', a more regularised form of exaction extorted by the army from the civilian population.

The accord terms for the surrender of towns varied considerably according to the political and military situation. Pappenheim secured the surrender of Hildesheim in September 1632 on 'most dishonourable conditions' since the city was 'strong and excellently well provided'. Out of 'his mere favour and grace' the garrison was to be no more than 2,000 men; the town was to pay over 200,000 reichsthaler in contributions, in return for which he would order 'strict military discipline'. Lutherans would be left in the free exercise of their religion. Since Pappenheim considered the citizens 'cowards who would endure anything', he ordered the seizure of all the silver plate in the city as the down payment for future contributions, and he ordered the seizure of all victuals and ammunition. Bernard of Saxe-Weimar secured the surrender of

Regensburg on 4 November 1633. This time the city had not been captured, but its walls had been breached and Saxe-Weimar maintained his own guard at the breach to secure compliance. The following day, the commander was allowed to march forth 'with bagge and baggage, their Armes, Drummes beating and Trumpets sounding' and escorted to Ingolstadt. Deserters from the Weimar forces were to be handed over, as were ammunition, ordnance and general provisions. When Gallas secured the surrender of Augsburg in March 1635, the accord allowed the general order of religion to remain as it had been in 1629 — that is after the implementation of the Edict of Restitution. The city was to pay the elector of Bavaria 400,000 reichsthaler 'for his expense in the warre' and there were other clauses concerning the legal recovery of goods and the right of the garrison to depart 'with flying colours, Drummes and fifes … bagge and baggage' in convoy to Erfurt.

That accord terms could lead to booty is evident from the experience of Hildesheim after its surrender to Pappenheim's forces. Freiburg changed hands six times and was also unsuccessfully besieged late in the war, but it seems to have escaped quite lightly from these experiences. In April 1634 the city was taken by the Swedes and plundered, as was customary after a place was taken by storm rather than surrendering. Poyntz noted that after a siege, probably of Weisskirchen, 'the execution continued the space of two howers, the pillageing two dayes', while Monro recalled that at Donauwörth 'the enemy were pitifully cut downe the most part of them in fury. The Town also was spoyled and quite plundered.' Booty taken in one theatre of battle might lead to retribution elsewhere. After the capture of Donauwörth, Monro noted that other towns requested safeguards from Gustavus Adolphus, 'in respect the Swedes were making great booty over all, where ever they came hanging the Papists by their purse, not sparing to torment their shinnes, as they [that is, the Catholics] did in Pomer[a]n[ia] and in the Markes of Brandenburg to the Protestants'.

There was civilian complicity even in this evident example of military excess. As Mortimer observes, 'the principal beneficiaries of the plundering were often not the soldiers, but the citizens of neighbouring towns who bought up the stolen goods for a fraction of their value from looters mainly interested in cash, either as a more portable form of booty or as the price of the next meal'. This civilian suffering and complicity is made quite explicit in the description of the sack of Magdeburg by Otto von Guericke, Burgomeister of the city:

… The most magnificent garments, hangings, silk stuffs, gold and silver lace, linen of all sorts, and other household goods were bought by the army sutlers for a mere song and peddled about by the cart load all through the archbishopric of Magdeburg and in Anhalt and Brunswick. Gold chains and rings, jewels, and every kind of gold and silver utensils were to be bought from the common soldiers for a tenth of their real value.

If for the soldier the war was, in the last analysis, his livelihood, the civilian was ultimately the paymaster. In Geoffrey Mortimer's phrase, 'contributions' were 'a euphemism for the extortion of resources in cash or kind from civilians to support the armies'. Since the security of food supply for men and animals was the single most important consideration, large battles tended to occur in August, by which time grain was ripening, permitting a large army to operate with greater freedom. Mid-winter campaigns by the French, for example, were rare and did not take place at all between 1643 and 1646. The Swedes were more adventurous, with the battle of Jankow taking place in early March 1645, but such campaigns were accompanied by high levels of attrition and were usually avoided. Few campaigns began before May, because of foraging problems: it was impossible to feed the cavalry horses before the grass was growing.

Once an army was able to secure unchallenged military control over a particular territory, the systematic extortion of contributions and other financial and material support resulted in the costs of warfare being sustained from the enemy economy. As David

Parrott observes: 'the war was no longer a struggle of attrition between [rival] powers, as one of the warring states was now shouldering the costs not only of its own army, but also a significant part of that of the enemy.' Gustavus Adolphus recognised this in his farewell speech to the Swedish Estates on 19 May 1630, before his departure for Germany. He said that he could:

well imagine the hardships which conscription entailed; yet if they would but consider it a little more closely it had great advantages too, since they had now these many years (thank God) been able with Swedish men to carry the war into the enemy's country, and so shift the burden of it to their foes.

The great advantage of the German war to outsiders such as Sweden and France was that highly mobile campaign armies 'could operate as self-financing entities, moving from one state to another extracting money by intimidation'.

If armies were to act in this way, then a premium was placed on intelligence gathering. Montecuccoli in *Concerning Battle (Sulle Battaglie)* emphasised 'the importance of intelligence data'. One contemporary commented ironically that 'a young woman from Leipzig or from Halle knows where the armies are in Germany, Hungary and other countries better than the politicians.' Generals had their own correspondents in various cities to provide them with intelligence on military matters, and if all else failed they could turn to the newspapers for such information. It was rare for armies to move forward on the basis of a rumour which in the end turned out to be false, though advances may have been unnecessarily delayed by incorrect information. The correspondence of generals such as Turenne was frequently intercepted. 'Of four letters that one writes in this country', he claimed in December 1644, 'three are lost.'

A successful battle invariably led to the capture of nearby towns. The two battles near Nördlingen, in 1634 and 1645, both resulted in the capture of the town, respectively by the victorious Imperial and French forces. We know most about the fate of towns in the Thirty Years' War, and Nordlingen is a particularly instructive example since it was so close to a number of important actions. Regardless as to whether the occupying force was Imperial, Swedish, Bavarian or French, the conditions of life remained similar: the occupying force demanded a constant flow of financial contributions as well as labour services to strengthen the city's fortifications. According to an estimate drawn up at the end of the century, the town had to pay over two million *florins* in war payments of various sorts in the course of the Thirty Years' War, with the peak in exactions in the early 1630s. Doubtless the city fathers chose to interpret payments made as widely as possible, so as to include exactions of cash, plate and so on; but there can be no doubt that there was a decline in the wealth of the citizenry in this period. Throughout the war the municipality had to prevent friction and disorder between the citizens and the soldiers and secure prompt payment of contributions by halting dissenting views, which they referred to as 'wicked, restless and irresponsible talk'.

Discontent was also held in check by the enormity of the crisis facing the citizens of Nördlingen. There had been an early experience of rapid inflation in the period of coinage debasement (known as the *Kipper- und Wipperzeit*) of early 1620s, and prices remained high long after the period of debasement ended in 1623. The number of citizen households fell by early half in the years between 1627 and 1640. Plague wreaked havoc in 1634, with the high point of the deaths in September and October, in the immediate aftermath of the crushing defeat of the Swedish forces and their allies. In the last four months of 1634 one-sixth of the entire community died. The death rate sextupled and 1,549 inhabitants of the city died in 1634, along with 300 refugees who were temporarily in the city. The plague continued to rage at precisely the moment that the Imperial army quartered hundreds of soldiers on the homes of the citizens and levied taxes of unprecedented severity.

Immigration could, and did, help restore the demographic balance. The plague of 1634 decimated households but many remarriages took place in the following years. In normal times immigration was discouraged; but in years of demographic disaster the rules were waived. Many of the immigrants came from other towns in southern Germany. The scale and complexity of population movement makes it very difficult to ascertain the total population loss in Germany during the Thirty Years' War. Displacement of the population rather than absolute population decline might seem an attractive theory for historians, but it is fairly clear that contemporaries would not have agreed: plague and war were perceived as linked phenomena. Perhaps by 'plague' they meant not just bubonic plague but other illnesses spread by human contact such as influenza, typhus and dysentery. Such 'plague' in a more generic sense was either associated with divine punishment for the war or was thought to be brought in the wake of the movements of huge armies. Various forms of illness such as influenza, typhus and dysentery falling upon a population weakened by war-induced malnutrition may well have killed more civilians than any strictly military depredations of the soldiery.

Rural affairs

The suffering of the countryside in the Thirty Years' War was greater than that of the towns. Rural communities could rarely defend themselves against anything more than a modest military strike; they could not easily resist the levy of contributions; and they were much more vulnerable to acts of wanton destruction, especially the adoption of a 'scorched earth' policy of depriving the enemy of possible material assistance. It was the scale of army desertion which transformed the problem faced by the rural communities. Army regiments were rarely up to strength. If the army served abroad, or the conditions of service deteriorated, desertion rates – except among veteran troops – were colossal. As David Parrott comments:

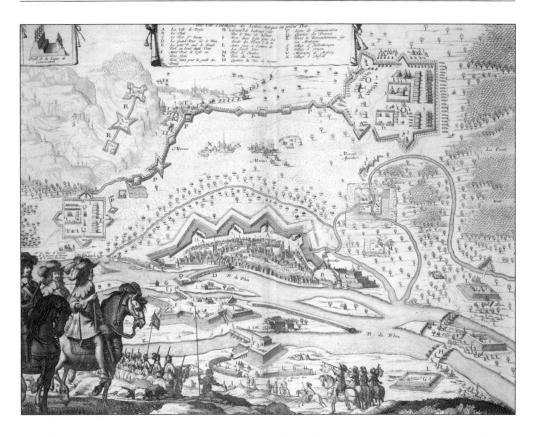

Siege of Breisach by Bernard of Saxe-Weimar, 1638. (British Library Museum)

desertion, whether in the form of spontaneous mass disbandment ... or the constant trickle of troops making their escape from hardship, inadequate food and pay and erratic military discipline, was not simply a challenge to the maintenance of military effectiveness. It also threatened to overwhelm the fragile mechanisms of local order, control and resource distribution. Only sustained mobilisation by rural communities could provide a mechanism for defence and this seems rarely to have occurred. Where peasant revolt did occur in the Thirty Years' War, it was directed against the exactions of a semi-permanent army of occupation and had an additional religious dimension to rally support.

The main focus of hostility in the revolt of the peasants in Austria in 1626 was the Bavarian army of occupation, which had been billeted on the country since 1620, when the Austrian estates had linked their cause to that of Bohemia in the movement against Ferdinand II. The presence of this army made the attempted restoration of Catholicism by

force a possibility. In October 1625, Lutheran peasant proprietors were required to convert to Catholicism by Easter the following year or to emigrate from Austria, suffering severe financial penalties. In the subsequent fighting, the Bavarian forces proved superior, though some noblemen assisted the rebellion, and by the spring of 1627, the revolt was suppressed. The imposition of Catholicism was resumed, though a movement of Protestant resistance remained, with the sacraments administered by itinerant lay preachers. Two further revolts, in 1632 and 1636, were on a much smaller scale. The Bavarian army of occupation had by then been withdrawn and these later revolts lacked the unifying focus of opposition it had provided. Wealthy peasants were the main supporters of the revolt of 1626–27; in the later rebellions, the participants were often landless labourers lacking the means or the cohesion to maintain the struggle.

Witness accounts

Incontestably, the most famous contemporary or near contemporary accounts of the Thirty Years' War derive from the three novels of Johann Jakob Christoph von Grimmelshausen, *The Adventures of Simplicissimus the German* (1668), *The Vagabond Courage* and *Springinsfeld* (both published in 1670). In Parker's words, these works 'have influenced decisively all historical study of the soldiers who fought the war, and their world' and, it may be added, characterised the relationship between military and civilian society. Since von Grimmelshausen had served as a soldier, it could reasonably be argued that his was a military, rather than a civilian account; however, by the time he began writing his novels, it was to supplement his peace-time income first as an innkeeper, later as steward to a physician, then once more as an innkeeper and finally as mayor of Renchen in the bishopric of Strasbourg. The military details of his novels, such as the account of the battle of Wittstock in 1636, were plagiarised, imaginary or at least unreliable. By the time of writing, his viewpoint had returned to that of the civilian who had to deal with the military, though he could share the viewpoint of the recruit who disliked and distrusted the officers.

What is particularly striking at the outset of *The Adventures of Simplicissimus the German* is von Grimmelshausen's depiction of 'the hatred that existed between soldiers and peasants' and between the lower orders of the army and the commanders. In the novel, this took the form of a dream:

On top of each tree sat a cavalier; and instead of bearing leaves the branches were decorated with all sorts of men. Some of these fellows had long pikes, others muskets, pistols,
halberds, small flags, and drums and fifes … The root was made up of lowly people like day-labourers, craftsmen, peasants, and such, who nevertheless gave the tree its strength and imparted vigour anew when it had been lost …. They were complaining about those sitting in the tree; and they had good cause, for the whole load rested on them and pressed them so hard that all their money was being squeezed out of their pockets and even out of the strongboxes which they had secured with seven locks …

The fiscal consequences of war, and how to pay for them, were an underlying preoccupation in many of the contemporary accounts. Another theme is that of the size of the impedimenta, 'the needless numbers of Women and Boys who follow Armies'. The boys, who often served as pages to as few as two soldiers, could add 50 per cent to the numbers and thus prove 'the very Vermine of an Army'. Female camp followers were considered more useful by Turner:

As woman was created to be a helper to man, so women are great helpers in Armies to their husbands, especially those of the lower condition; … they provide, buy and dress their husbands meat when their husbands are on duty, or newly come from it, they bring in fewel [sic] for fire, and wash their linens; … especially they are useful in Camps and Leaguers, being permitted (which should be not be refused them) to go some miles from the Camp to buy Victuals and other Necessaries.

In a remarkable study, Geoffrey Mortimer has identified more than 70 eyewitness accounts of the Thirty Years' War. Many were not written by civilians; others, which purport to be civilian eyewitnesses may not have been so, or may only have witnessed some of the incidents they recorded. Philip Vincent's publication *The Lamentations of Germany* (1638) included a report on the 'miserable estate of Germany' from the refugee G. R. Weckerlin which was a catalogue of horrors and atrocities. It appears Weckerlin was an eyewitness of the siege of Heidelberg, but was otherwise reliant on what he had heard 'from sufficient testimonies'. His account had moral and polemical intentions, stressing the 'miserable condition' of Germany, which was interpreted as 'the full effects of sinne'.

Three other contemporary witnesses highlighted by Mortimer are closer to fact than some of the fantasy reproduced by Vincent. One is a nun, Juliana Ernst, whose account of the events leading up to the attack on Villingen in 1633 is judged by Mortimer 'in many respects the best-developed narrative in the texts

studied'. A second source discussed by Mortimer is the chronicle covering the years from 1613 to 1660 composed by the Freiburg priest, Thomas Mallinger. Mallinger's account was a war chronicle superimposed on a mundane diary he already kept. Gallus Zembroth provides us with a third contemporary chronicle discussed by Mortimer. The mayor of Allensbach in alternate years from 1632 to 1652, Zembroth, a leading landowner in the area, recorded the war experiences of the village and its neighbourhood from 1632 until the final departure of troops in 1649. 'The most prominent theme in his account is the cost to the village of contributions imposed by the military,' comments Mortimer:

It is evident from his account that a system of municipal taxation spread the burden of contributions, and despite grumbling he never suggests that the villagers were unable to pay. Even when the costs of the first year of peace

proved greater than those of the years of war a
modest loan tided them over

Zembroth's aim was to record the
hardships of his community. In Mortimer's
judgement: 'dire events were few and spread
over a long period, atrocities were virtually
non-existent, and … although undoubtedly
exploited, the Allensbachers were able to
keep their heads above water within a
functioning economic system throughout
the war period.'

Do the contemporary accounts disprove
the prevailing interpretation of the Thirty
Years' War as a particularly destructive
conflict, especially from the point of view of
civilians? Many of the accounts mention the
sack of Magdeburg in 1631, which was
totally destroyed along with its population.
This was depicted in terms which suggest
recognition that this, even by the standards
of German conflict, was a particularly
gruesome event. Monro laments in passing
'the losse of many poore soules within

Jacques Callot (1592–1635): *The revenge of the peasants*
(from the Miseries of War). (Roger-Viollet)

Madeburg, being cut off by the crueltie of
Generall Tillies Armie, having su[r]pr[ise]d
the Towne that was never taken before,
sparing neither man, woman nor childe,
but putting all alike cruelly to death, and in
the end, the Towne was burnt downe.'
However, it is clear from the frequent
mention of Magdeburg that it was seen as
the exception rather than the norm.

The war in pictures: Jacques Callot's 'Miseries of War'

The illustrations, documents and accounts
of Matthäus Merian and Johann Philipp
Abele (Abelin) in the *Theatrum Europaeum*,
which was produced in Frankfurt, at the
centre of the German publishing trade
tended to emphasise the journalistic
perspective of the war. In Mortimer's words:
'atrocities and destruction were featured,
while stability and regeneration were
overlooked and the everyday was ignored.'
The regional diversity of Germany makes
a balanced account of the civilian suffering
in the Thirty Years' War extraordinarily
difficult to achieve.

But its visual depiction is unforgettable,
above all because of the remarkable
engravings by the Lorraine artist Jacques
Callot. Today Callot is famous for what are
seen as the epitome of the anti-war visual
tracts of the seveenth century, the great
and small 'Misères et malheurs de la guerre',
which were probably completed *c.*1632–33.
In fact he gained his reputation from the
depiction of the capture of Breda in 1625.
The same eye for detail, on a much smaller
scale, was revealed in the *Miseries of War*
cycle. Each illustration in the cycle tells its
own powerful story about the civilian
sufferings of war, but perhaps the most
representative are 'The revenge of the
peasants' (a murderous attack on some
soldiers separated from their troop) and
'The pillage and burning of a village'. Callot

ABOVE Jacques Callot (1592–1635): 'The pillage and burning of a village' (from the *Miseries of War*). (AKG, Berlin)

BELOW Jacques Callot (1592–1635): 'The pillage of a farm' (from the *Miseries of War*). (AKG, Berlin)

reveals in visual representation the reality of that 'hatred that existed between soldiers and peasants' described by von Grimmelshausen.

Negotiating for the future

The official opening of the Congress of Westphalia was on 11 July 1643. The first concrete French and Swedish demands were issued on 11 June 1645. A preliminary treaty between the emperor and France was signed on 13 September 1646, but the definitive treaty was signed on 24 October 1648. By any reckoning, peace had been an unconscionable time coming. Peacemaking has to take account of events on the battlefield; or, to put it another way, military events happening at the end of a war may have a disproportionate effect on treaty making. Mazarin wrote of the emperor's power that 'one single accident of the kind that occurs ever day in military affairs is capable of ruining his grandeur forever and putting him in a state from which he will not be able to recover.' The defeat at Zusmarhausen in May 1648 and the pressure brought about by the Swedish siege of Prague meant that it was unlikely that Ferdinand III could gain great advantage from the last phase of the Westphalian negotiations in 1648. Yet though concessions might have to be made in Germany, the emperor was determined to salvage as much authority as possible within the Austrian homelands (the *Erbländer*). France was weakened by a royal minority (Louis XIV, born September 1638, was only 10 years' old) and the political upheaval known as the Fronde; nevertheless Louis de Condé managed to avert military and political disaster by winning the battle of Lens in July 1648.

Because of their foreign origins, neither Mazarin nor Anne of Austria who was mother and Regent of Louis XIV, could risk making a disadvantageous peace settlement; but all the same they sought peace as a matter of urgency, which was interpreted by Philip IV as an indication of weakness. The Spanish government based its hopes on dissension in France during the royal minority, and sought to make a separate peace with the Dutch. The French plenipotentiaries were convinced rebellion in France was likely: the duc de Longueville predicted its timing, which was particularly ironic given that he was one of the participants in the uprising of January 1649. The idea of exchanging French-held Catalonia for the Spanish Netherlands as part of the terms of a Franco-Spanish marriage alliance had been accepted by Mazarin as a condition of peace as early as September 1645. The Spanish plenipotentiaries deliberately revealed the terms of the impending peace to the Dutch, on the (correct) assumption that pro-peace sentiment in the United Provinces would soar. The Dutch were hardly likely to be enthusiastic supporters for replacing a weak Spanish regime on the southern border with a strong French one: they quoted the maxim 'the Frenchman as your friend but not your neighbour'. A balance of power principle was operating in practice if not consciously, when the Dutch made peace with Spain in 1648 because of their fear of a prospective French hegemony. The French capture of Dunkirk on 11 October 1646 had been one victory too many, and one too close to home, for the Dutch to accept.

Mazarin made peace with ~~the~~ Ferdinand III on 24 October 1648, much against his inclination, because of the fear that Sweden would defect from the French alliance much as the Dutch had done. He would have preferred to continue the German conflict until Spain made peace. Why had France, a state of nearly 20 million people, failed to

Royal minority in France, 1643–51. Louis XIV, King of France (1638–1715; king from 1643), by Henri Testelin. (Ann Ronan Picture Library)

conquer more territory than Sweden, whose population was one-tenth that of France? Derek Croxton concludes that the obvious reason was that the empire was only a secondary theatre of war for France; French commitments there were kept as low as possible, so as to concentrate most of the war effort against Spain in the Low Countries, where significant successes were achieved in the late 1640s. Seen against this perspective, the French gains in 1648 – the transfer of the various parts of Alsace, the Sundgau, Breisach, a garrison in Philippsburg and the formal recognition of French possession of Metz, Toul and Verdun– represent a significant achievement, close to the highest French hopes rather than the lowest.

Yet almost immediately after the Peace of Westphalia, Mazarin was criticised in France for not making peace with Spain at the same time: 'some accused him of not being interested in peace and thus demanding too difficult terms, while others felt that he was leaving France vulnerable to intervention from the Austrian Habsburgs in her continuing war with Spain.' The notoriously bad relations between the plenipotentiaries, chiefly between Servien and d'Avaux, received full attention during the Fronde and helped fuel the accusations that Mazarin was

a warmonger who had an 'aversion to peace'. The secret conduct of the negotiations; the fact that Brienne – secretary of state for foreign affairs – counted for little and the main correspondence was between Mazarin and Servien; and, above all, that the opportunity for a general peace seemed to have been lost by a conscious act of policy in 1648 — these disparate pieces of information were pieced together by Longueville and d'Avaux as evidence for their campaign to discredit the chief minister. Louis de Condé's insistence on the dismissal of Servien, Lionne and Le Tellier during Mazarin's first exile in the summer of 1651 was the final verdict on the mechanism by which the chief minister had maintained his power and influence over the Regent. During the Westphalian negotiations, Lionne used his influence to support Servien, his uncle, against the other two plenipotentiaries.

It was the resurgence of Swedish military power in Germany in the 1640s which had made that alliance so critical for France, but which in turn gave Christina of Sweden's negotiators the capacity to block a settlement which did not conform to Sweden's interests. The Swedes received the western half of Pomerania, together with land in the eastern part, notably Stettin, Rügen, Wismar and the bishoprics of Bremen and Verden, which they had taken from the Danes in the 1643–45 war. In recompense for the loss of half of Pomerania – which should have passed to Brandenburg upon the death of the last duke in 1637 – Frederick-William of Brandenburg Prussia received the secularised bishoprics of Halberstadt, Minden and Camin. He was also to receive the expectancy of the bishopric of Magdeburg, less four areas ceded to John George of Saxony upon the death of its current administrator. 'Contentment of the soldiery' had been a primary goal of Swedish policy at the Congress of Westphalia. The Swedish army, not trusting the government, sent a plenipotentiary to the congress to protect its interests. These efforts were rewarded by a payment of five million *reichsthaler* to the unpaid Swedish troops.

The five years spent in negotiations between 1643 and 1648 made the Westphalian peace congress the longest in early modern and modern European history. One explanation for the long delay was the complexity of the issues at stake: German religious and political issues; the demands of the foreign powers, especially France and Sweden; and the negotiating strength or otherwise of the emperor Ferdinand III and Philip IV of Spain and the skill of their plenipotentiaries (respectively Trauttsmannsdorff and Peñaranda). For example, Mazarin believed that Philip IV instructed Peñaranda to break off negotiations in 1648 in the expectation that the disappointed hopes of peace would lead to civil disorder in France.

Equally important, however, was the fact that the fighting continued during the peace negotiations; there was no preceding truce or armistice. This was specifically repudiated by Mazarin: 'His Majesty and his allies do not envisage reducing the fire of war by a truce but extinguishing it totally by means of a good peace.' A practical consideration drove

Christina and her council in Sweden to reject the idea of an armistice: 'we find an armistice insufficient for our needs; it is moreover dangerous and would provide our troops with an opportunity to mutiny.' Emperor Ferdinand III had a further practical reason for avoiding a truce. In his case, he feared that any cessation of military operations, especially one which ended in a failure at the negotiating table, would make it extremely difficult for him to mobilise opinion in favour of a resumption of war among his German allies. It seems only Maximilian of Bavaria felt that a truce was relevant and this was simply to avoid further ravaging of his duchy. While the emperor waited on military events between 1644 and 1646 before deciding to make concessions to France, the anti-Habsburg allies did not use their military advantage to increase their demands or any military setback to reduce them. 'The loss of two or three thousand men [in battle]', Servien declared in May 1645, 'neither modifies the plans nor alters the destiny of a great kingdom.' Nevertheless, Mazarin used a gambling image to describe French policy in July 1646: it was better to 'quit them game when winning, because you can assure yourself of your gains and count on what you already hold'. This became a pressing necessity once the prospect of internal civil disorder in France became a reality in the summer and autumn of 1648.

Only the emperor could make the concessions which would satisfy one of the parties and ensure that the other would, in its own right, accept terms and make peace. Unlike the French, the Austrian Habsburg plenipotentiaries did not display internal rivalries and disagreements, because Trauttsmannsdorf's primacy was accepted by his colleagues: he had been nominated as chief plenipotentiary as early as 1633. Ferdinand III would have preferred separate peace negotiations. Having accepted a

Frederick William, the 'Great Elector' of Brandenburg Prussia (1620–88; elector from 1640). (Ann Ronan Picture Library)

Nuremberg (1649–50) and the end of the war: Karl Gustav (the future King Charles X of Sweden) and Ottavio Piccolomini, the Imperial commander, settle the terms for demobilising the armies in Germany. (Roger-Viollet)

congress, he sought to come to a compromise peace with France and Sweden and leave the internal affairs of the empire to a separate negotiation. Finally, on 29 August 1645, he accepted a limitation on his prerogative by allowing the German estates to be fully represented in the congress at Westphalia. Secret instructions were issued to Trauttsmannsdorff on 16 October 1645, which determined the form of the emperor's final concessions. In summary, these were consistent with Imperial policy after the disastrous setback at Breitenfeld in 1631: withdrawal from the empire as an active participant might be acceptable to the emperor if the religious settlement was reserved to the Imperial estates themselves; above all, there could be no concessions of either a religious or a confessional kind within the hereditary lands. There was, however, no longer any question of an 'Imperial absolutism' for Germany, even at the back of Trauttsmannsdorff's mind. After 1631, the *Reichsabsolutismus of Ferdinand II*, even if it had existed in embryonic form before 1629, was definitively abandoned.

In the end, negotiations with France were a higher priority than those with Sweden: France was at least a Catholic kingdom and therefore a less dangerous adversary. Maximilian of Bavaria insisted that France must be ceded significant parts of Alsace as the price of avoiding his defection from the Habsburg alliance. Ferdinand III refused to contemplate the cession of Strasbourg, but was prepared to offer the Habsburg patrimony of Upper Alsace. Finally, a preliminary accord was reached with France on 13 September 1646. This was largely the product of Maximilian of Bavaria's insistence on excluding Spain's interests from the negotiations, and putting the defence of Bavaria and the German estates higher than the retention of all the Habsburg patrimonial

lands. However, Ferdinand III and his successors never lost the ambition of recovering Upper Alsace.

The emperor signed a preliminary peace with Sweden on 18 February 1647, which was a comparable document to the preliminary settlement with France the previous September. The demands of the Swedish soldiery provided an additional complication, however, and though they did receive a financial indemnity some Swedish troops remained in Germany until the indemnity was paid in full, that is, until 1652.

A final difficulty in the negotiations was provided by the later demand of France – following the conclusion of a separate peace between Spain and the United Provinces in January 1648 – that the empire should be neutral in any continuing Franco-Spanish conflict. In the end, even this demand had to be conceded by Ferdinand III, though he did succeed in achieving two things. He preserved the Imperial Constitution from being remodelled in the interests of France or Sweden, even though it was to be modified. He also defended the work of the Counter-Reformation in the Austrian homelands — although this was at the price of concessions to the German Protestant princes. A war-weary Germany finally accepted that peace had come, and two series of celebrations were organised, the first on the conclusion of the settlements in 1648 and early 1649, the other in 1650 after the Recess of Nuremberg made the Peace of Westphalia a law of the empire and finally secured the departure of the Swedish soldiery. In total 178 separate celebrations were held in the Holy Roman empire, while fireworks accompanied the Recess of Nuremberg.

A permanent settlement?

That this Peace and Amity be observ'd and cultivated with such a Sincerity and Zeal, that each Party shall endeavour to procure the Benefit, Honour and Advantage of the other; that thus on all sides they may see this Peace and Friendship in the Roman empire, and the kingdom of France flourish, by entertaining a good and faithful Neighbourhood.

The preamble of the Franco-Imperial Peace Treaty of 24 October 1648 makes clear that a permanent peace between the warring sides was envisaged. What would be called today 'confidence building measures' were necessary so that a fragile settlement might become secure and enduring. For this reason, many of the details of the separate Suedo– Imperial Peace Treaty and the treaty concerning the Estates of the empire were included within the terms of the Franco-Imperial Peace. The result was a complex interlocking set of documents constituting the Westphalian 'settlement', a settlement which is not easy to evaluate.

For France, there remained a residual fear of the Habsburg cousins, the emperor and the king of Spain, acting in collusion at its expense. Richelieu had conceived the concept of collective security. In 1658 Mazarin belatedly convinced some German states to join a French-dominated League of the Rhine. But, in general, the German states rejected such an idea: the Peace of Westphalia was a definitive settlement. As a result, collective security should not be necessary. However, as a result of the treaty, the princes had gained territorial superiority, though not sovereignty over their states. They were not supposed to use this increase in prerogative power at the expense of the emperor or the empire, but in practice they could, and did, enter into foreign

alliances at their whim. The abandonment of the French alliance by the Great Elector, Frederick William of Brandenburg Prussia, at the end of the Dutch War in 1679 is one example. Emperor Leopold I (1640–1705 emperor from 1658) was asked to defend the empire in 1674 against French aggression, demonstrating the possibility of Imperial power making a 'come back', precisely because the threat to the balance of power was perceived to be France rather than the alliance of the Spanish and Austrian Habsburgs.

Conflict resolution in Germany

Within Germany, three problems remained to be resolved after 1648. The first was that of 'peace', both acquiring it and preserving it, and above all dealing with all the litigation that arose from the 30 years of warfare. There was supposed to be an amnesty. Article II of the Treaty of Westphalia was clear on the overwhelming need to forget the past:

That there shall be on the one side and the other a perpetual Oblivion, Amnesty, or Pardon of all that has been committed since the beginning of these Troubles … all that has pass'd on the one side, and the other, as well before as during the War, in Words, Writings, and Outrageous Actions, in Violences, Hostilitys, Damages and Expences, without any respect to Persons or Things, shall be entirely abolish'd in such a manner that all that might be demanded of, or pretended to, by each other on that behalf, shall be bury'd in eternal Oblivion.

There were, however, many disputes over the nature of the amnesty and how it should be interpreted. After 1648, when matters came before the Imperial Diet, a joint resolution of Catholics (*Corpus Catholicorum*) and Protestants (*Corpus Evangelicorum*, that is Lutherans and Calvinists) acting collectively was necessary. Litigation arising from the war proliferated and was very much a product of the time, but the idea of an 'eternal oblivion', that in forgiving lies the substance of peace (*in amnestia consista substantia pacis*), has modern resonance.

The second problem was that of internal political and constitutional adjustments. An eighth electorate was created for Bavaria and this allowed the restitution of the confiscated electoral title to the Palatinate. In turn, this set a precedent for further adjustments to the Imperial constitution, especially in the sensitive area of the religious balance of the electors who played the decisive role in voting for the next emperor under the terms of the Golden Bull of 1356. In order to retain his loyalty during the War of the Spanish Succession, the Elector of Brandenburg Prussia was given the title of king in Prussia in 1701. A ninth electorate, this time for Hanover, was created for similar reasons in 1692, during the War of the League of Augsburg.

The idea of an immutable constitution of the Holy Roman empire was thus abandoned in 1648, though no- one would have suspected the scale of the changes that might result in the long- term. Moreover, the religious boundaries between Catholics and Protestants were not fixed, in spite of 1624 being adopted as the 'standard year' for the possession of secularised church lands. The conversion of the electors of the Palatinate and Saxony to Catholicism, respectively in 1685 and 1697, altered the religious balance of the electors and further strengthened the Catholic majority.

The third problem to be addressed was how to overcome the economic damage of war and create a climate of security for economic progress. The state, at the level of the principality, had to encourage immigration, and to do this a policy of religious toleration was advantageous: in this respect, the policy of Brandenburg Prussia was more realistic than that of Saxony. The

development of 'Cameralism' – the theory of increasing the economic and fiscal power of the German 'state'– in both Catholic and Protestant principalities was a response to the urgent need to rebuild the economic capacities and population resources of the state after the Thirty Years' War. Leopold I's economic adviser, Johan Joachim Becher (1635–82), was a populationist who argued that consumers' expenditure generates income. Wilhelm von Schröder (1640–88) – heavily influenced by the English school of 'political arithmetic' – argued that the crown's tax revenue should rise in relation to the increase in wealth that would follow from a prosperous economy. Finally, Philipp Wilhelm von Hörningk (1638–1714) argued in *Austria above all, when it so wishes* (1684) that the Austrian hereditary lands could support double their existing level of population.

Clearly some German states were better able than others to attract immigrants and rebuild their economies. The ease with which substantial mercenary armies had been recruited in the Thirty Years' War, at least down to the early 1630s, suggested an alternative, or at least complementary, policy that might be followed: that of developing a high 'army to population' ratio, in other words making the state proportionally more militarised than its rivals. Some of these troops could be hired out abroad as a source of income to the state. In the eighteenth century, Hesse, which had played a secondary but not insignificant role in the later stages of the Thirty Years' War, had an army size larger in relation to its population than Prussia. When the British recruited Hessian mercenaries, it had the effect of subsidising the Hessian taxpayer, whose per capita fiscal burden was half that of his Prussian counterpart and actually fell in the course of the eighteenth century.

Conclusions

The Peace of Westphalia left Germany as a profoundly militarised society, with a strong

potential for internecine conflict. It was a
tribute to the peacemakers of the 1640s that
it was a century before that potential was
fully realised. It was not until 1740 that the
Prussian pre-emptive strike against Silesia
precipitated the War of the Austrian
Succession and the first of a series of
struggles between Prussia and Austria for the
leadership of the empire, which culminated
in the war of 1866. Many publicists,
including Samuel Puffendorf and Abraham
de Wicquefort, were fascinated by the
German empire as it emerged from the
Thirty Years' War. Part of the attraction,
writes Maurice Keens-Soper:

*was that it ceasing to be a body politic and
becoming an association of states. Although still
attached by ties of common inheritance, its
principal members were increasingly incorporated
in the wider European order of independent
states …*

For Puffendorf, writing in 1675, a states-
system was one in which 'several states are
connected as to seem to constitute one body
but whose members retain sovereignty'. In
Puffendorf's definition, the European states-
system governed by diplomatic procedure
was further developed or promoted by the
Westphalian settlement. De Wicquefort noted
that the would-be German states paid more
attention to issues of representation,
recognition, rank, precedence, ritual and
ceremony than to striking the bargains that
eventually resulted in the terms of the
Münster and Osnabrück settlements.
   The Peace of Westphalia in 1648 was an
incomplete peace, and not the general
European peace settlement that the
plenipotentiaries had envisaged. It failed to
end the war between France and Spain: their
conflict lasted until the Peace of the Pyrenees
in 1659. The Westphalian settlement marked
in only an incomplete form the shift in the
balance of power from a Spanish Habsburg
to a Bourbon preponderance in Europe.
If Mazarin's greatest diplomatic
accomplishments were indeed the Peace of
Westphalia in 1648 and the Peace of the

Pyrenees in 1659, as Derek Croxton recalls,
'national aggrandisement' rather than
defensible borders was his guiding purpose;
Alsace was 'more of a defensive hindrance
than a benefit' in this process. Rather than
securing permanent peace for Europe, the
ambiguities and unfinished business of these
treaties provided both pretext and
opportunity for Louis XIV's grand designs for
European hegemony, which by 1672 had
completely overturned the traditional policy
of Richelieu and Mazarin in seeking to build
an alliance system against the Habsburgs.
   The emergence of a stronger France,
which might pose a threat to the balance of
power in Europe, was not a rapid or
inevitable process. The ending of the alliance
with the Dutch Republic and Sweden in
1648 meant that French power on its own
had to confront Spain and, during the
Fronde, Philip IV's armies made steady
progress against those of Louis XIV. A
reliable new ally to take on a military role,
as Sweden had in the 1640s, was needed. It
took time for Mazarin to decide that the
English Protectorate – because of its
revolutionary origins and apparent Puritan
credentials – was right for this role. Yet once
the military pact was formed between
Mazarin and Cromwell in 1657, the crucial
breakthrough of Turenne at the battle of the
Dunes on 14 June 1658, was achieved
rapidly and the treaty with Spain followed
relatively quickly. Yet the Peace of the
Pyrenees was, if anything, even more
ambiguous as a treaty than that of
Westphalia, and the cause of further war
rather than the prelude to sustained peace.
   Historians have nevertheless seen 1648 as
a watershed in one important respect: 'the
Treaty of Westphalia did not stop the
enforcement of uniformity within particular
territories,' John Coffey argues, 'it simply
signalled an end to confessional wars
between different states.' There could be no
return to a single, unified, Christendom.
Pope Innocent X denounced the concessions
to Protestantism in November 1648. But the
Papacy had been excluded, in spite of the
presence of Fabio Chigi, future Pope

Battle of the Dunes, 14 June 1658. Turenne leads the French cavalry charge. (Ann Ronan Picture Library)

Alexander VII, at the negotiations. In the new European 'states system' confessional alliances were to be a thing of the past, or nearly so. It is true that at times Louis XIV tried to project the alliance of the Maritime Powers (England and the United Provinces) between 1689 and 1713, as a Protestant alliance against Catholicism. But there was no simple Protestant versus Catholic alliance system after Westphalia, for all the fears of a further outbreak of confessional warfare. In this respect, the French policy in the course of the Thirty Years' War – though not in the period of Louis XIV's rule after 1661 – of seeking a non-confessional alliance system to secure a balance of power had been strikingly 'modern'. It may have been controversial to Cardinal Richelieu's hard-line Catholic opponents at the time, but Louis XIII's successful alliance system in the Thirty Years' War was a portent for future diplomatic alignments, which have tended to be based more on the communities of interest of states than on confessional or ideological uniformity.

Further reading

Abelin, J. and Merian, M. *Theatrum Europæum, oder ausfürliche … Beschreibung aller … Geschichten … vom Jahr Christi 1617…* (multiple volumes, various edns. Frankfurt, 1647 etc.)

Anon. *The Modern History of the World, Or, An Historicall Relation of the Most Memorable passages in Germany and elsewhere since the beginning of this present yeere 1635. VIII,* (London, 1635).

Asch, R. G. *The Thirty Years War: the Holy Roman Empire and Europe, 1618–1648* (Basingstoke/New York 1997).

Barker, T. M. *The Military Intellectual and Battle. Raimondo Montecuccoli and the Thirty Years' War* (Albany, NY, 1975).

Bély J. *L'Europe des traités de Westphalie. Esprit de la diplomatie et diplomatie de l'esprit* (Paris, 2000).

Bonney, R. J. (ed.) *The Rise of the Fiscal State in Europe, c.1200–1815* (Oxford, 1999).

Bonney, R. J. 'Early modern theories of state finance', *Economic Systems and State Finance*, ed. Bonney (Oxford, 1995).

Bonney, R. J. 'The European Reaction to the Trial and Execution of Charles I', *The Regicides and the Execution of the Charles I,* ed. J. Peacey (London, 2001), 247–279.

Bonney, R. J. 'The Forging and Relinquishing of Protestant Identities: Religion and Politics in Britain and Germany since the Reformation', *Religion and Politics in Britain and Germany*, Bonney, R J Bosbach, K and Brockmann, T (eds) (Prince Albert Studies, 19, Munich, 2001)

Bonney, R J 'The struggle for great power status…' *Economic Systems and State Finance*, ed. Bonney (Oxford 1995).

Bonney, R J *The Limits of Absolutism in ancien regime France* (Aldershot, 1995).

Coffey, J R D *Persecution and Toleration in Protestant England, 1558–1689* (Harlow, 2000).

Croxton, D., *Peacemaking in Early Modern Europe. Cardinal Mazarin and the Congress of Westphalia, 1643–1648.* (Selingsgrove, 1999).

Friedrichs, C R *Urban Society in An Age of War: Nördlingen, 1580–1720* (Princeton, NJ, 1979).

Goodrick, A T S (ed) *The Relation of Sydnam Poyntz, 1624–1636*, Camden Society, (London, 1908).

Guthrie, W P *Battles of the Thirty Years War: from White Mountain to Nördlingen, 1618–1635* (Contributions in military studies no. 213. Westport, Ct; Greenwood Press, London 2002). A second volume will follow to complete the analysis to 1648. The single most important work on the military history of the Thirty Years' War to date.

Lynn, J A *Giant of the Grand Siècle: the French Army, 1610–1715* (Cambridge, 1997).

Monro, R *His Expedition with the Worthy Scots Regiment called Mac-Keys,.* Brockington, Jnr W S (ed.) (Westport, Conn. and London, 1999).

Mortimer, G 'Did contemporaries recognize a "Thirty Years' War"?', *English Historical Review*, 116 (2001), 124–136.

Parker, N G (ed.), *The Thirty Years' War*, 2nd rev. edn. (London, 1997).

Parrott, D *Richelieu's Army: War, Government, and Society in France, 1624–1642* (Cambridge, 2001).

Rebel, H *Peasant Classes: the Bureaucratization of Property and Family Relations under Early Habsburg Absolutism, 1511–1636* (Princeton, NJ, 1983).

Roberts M (ed.), *Sweden as a Great Power, 1611–1697. Government, Society, Foreign Policy* (London, 1968).

Roberts, M., *Gustavus Adolphus: a History of Sweden, 1611–1632* (repr., 2 vols., London, 1963–8).

Steinberg, S. H., *The 'Thirty Years' War' and the conflict for European hegemony, 1600–1660* (London, 1966).

Sutherland, N. M., 'The origins of the Thirty Years' War and the structure of European politics', *English Historical Review*, 107 (1992), 587–625.

Turner, Sir James, Pallas Armata. *Military Essayes of the Ancient Grecian, Roman and Modern Art of War. Written in the Years 1670 and 1671* (repr. New York, 1968).

von Grimmelshausen, J J C *Simplicius Simplicissimus*, trans. G. Schulz-Behrend (Indianapolis, New York, Kansas City, repr. 1965).

Wicquefort, A de *The Embassador and his Functions*, trans. J. Digby, London, 1716; ed. M. Keens-Soper (University of Leicester, Centre for the Study of Diplomacy, 1997).

Web resources

At the time of going to press, the Abelin/Merian *Theatrum Europeaum* was in the process of being digitized and placed on the web:
www.digbib.bibliothek.uni-augsburg.de/1/index.html/

There is a remarkable website of images relating to the Peace of Westphalia:
www.muenster.de/stadt/kongress1648/04_kongress/index.html and pages nearby

Working papers of a conference on 1648 — War and Peace in Europe:
www.lwl.org/westfaelischer-friede/wfe-t/wfe-txt1-30.htm and pages nearby

Chronology of the war by C. Atkinson:
www.pipeline.com/~cwa/Index.htm

The website of the Fine Arts Museums of San Francisco (www.search.famsf.org) has a collection of 667 images of Callot in digitized form, including the images cited.

For those who are really 'into' the military history of the time, there is the REMPAS (Renaissance, Early Modern Pike and Shot) discussion list, which has some important material placed on it, particularly by Daniel Stalberg:
www.groups.yahoo.com/group/REMPAS/

Index

Related titles from Osprey Publishing

To order any of these titles, or for more information on Osprey Publishing, contact:

Osprey Direct (UK) Tel: +44 (0)1933 443863 Fax: +44 (0)1933 443849 E-mail: info@ospreydirect.co.uk
Osprey Direct (USA) c/o MBI Publishing Toll-free: 1 800 826 6600 Phone: 1 715 294 3345
Fax: 1 715 294 4448 E-mail: info@ospreydirectusa.com

www.ospreypublishing.com

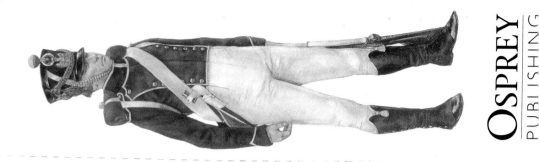

FIND OUT MORE ABOUT OSPREY

❏ Please send me a FREE trial issue of Osprey Military Journal

❏ Please send me the latest listing of Osprey's publications

❏ I would like to subscribe to Osprey's e-mail newsletter

Title/rank _____

Name _____

Address _____

_____

_____

Postcode/zip _____

State/country _____

E-mail _____

Which book did this card come from?

_____

❏ I am interested in military history

My preferred period of military history is _____

❏ I am interested in military aviation

My preferred period of military aviation is _____

I am interested in *(please tick all that apply)*

❏ general history   ❏ militaria   ❏ model making

❏ wargaming   ❏ re-enactment

Please send to:

USA & Canada:
Osprey Direct USA, c/o MBI Publishing,
PO Box 1, 729 Prospect Ave, Osceola, WI 54020, USA

UK, Europe and rest of world:
Osprey Direct UK, PO Box 140, Wellingborough,
Northants, NN8 2FA, United Kingdom

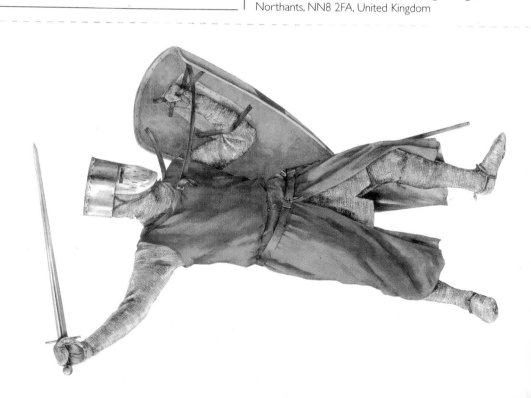

PUBLISHING

www.ospreypublishing.com

call our telephone hotline
for a free information pack

USA & Canada: 1-800-826-6600
UK, Europe and rest of world call:
+44 (0) 1933 443 863

Young Guardsman
Figure taken from *Warrior 22:
Imperial Guardsman 1799–1815*
Published by Osprey
Illustrated by Christa Hook

Knight, c.1190
Figure taken from *Warrior 1: Norman Knight 950 – 1204AD*
Published by Osprey
Illustrated by Christa Hook

POSTCARD